# MARRIAGE MASALA

## Rod & Ruthie Gilbert

**MARRIAGE MASALA**
**52 Spices For A Healthy Marriage**
Revised 2011 Edition
Copyright @2004 Rod & Ruthie Gilbert
Email: r2gilberto@yahoo.com

**Published by:**
**Elemental Publishing LLC**
175 W Monroe St #131
Wytheville VA 24382
info@elementalpub.com

ISBN: 978-1-935614-99-9

Printed In USA For World Wide Distribution (excluding India)

Unless otherwise specified, all Scripture quotations are taken from, New International version copyright© 1978 by New York International Bible Society.

**For more copies write to :**

**175 W Monroe St 131**
**Wytheville VA 24382**
**info@elementalpub.com**

Dedication

To

Luke and Kirti; Ben and Shiyani; Dan and Michelle ; Prilla and Joe

whose love for each other spices us with delight and to

Ande

for his unique way of giving us all so much life,hope and fun;

a great 'Masala Family.'

# Acknowledgements

Our special love and thanks to our many friends and resource couples who continue to carry the 'family ministry' baton across the world.

In particular we thank Joel and Carol, Vasanth and Prenita, Jacob and Rani, Rajasing and Gnanam, Dr. and Dr Mrs. Harris, Vasanthi and Sheldon, Don and Anita, Jaykaran and Kavitha, Peterand Sally, Megella and Rampart, Tim and Karol, and Wilfred and Shanti,who inspired us to write this book initially.

We deeply appreciate all the couples who have dared to share their marriages with us. As we relive their joys and pains through this book, we have been careful to protect their identity; all names have been changed - we send them our love and we delight in them all.

A big thankyou to our original team who have made 'Marriage Masala' a reality.

**Serena:** a superb editor, with her insights in re-writing and her encouragement, love and laughter.

**Graham and Nadine**: the artists, who bring the spices alive with sensitivity and humour generously giving their skills and time as a gift.

**Annie:** the graphic designer for giving such a superb flavour of masala on the cover.

**Betty:** and the Marriage Masala intercession team: soaking us constantly in prayer.

**Anne and Shelly:** For endless hours on their computers.

And now to - **Brad and Paige:** the publishers of this new edition- For their enthusiastic adoption of the vision!

# Introduction

## 52 spices for a healthy marriage!

This is a book of 52 'spices' one for every week of the year to give fun and inspiration
to any couple willing to skillfully blend the masalas. Our strap line is 'To make good marriages tastier!' We believe this is a never-ending process, so Marriage Masala can be appropriate for anyone whether they have been married for 5 months, 5 years, or even 55 years. Marriage Masala is a collection of 'spices' -skills-offered to couples, to blend into their marriages to improve and to enrich family life, just as they would grind spices into the masalas of their curries to make them tastier. The spices have been collected from the experiences we have gained in our marriage of 35 years, and from bringing up 5 children, and in running a host of seminars at Scripture Union's Family Life Centre at Cornerstone House, Mahabalipuram, South India, and at many other locations worldwide, since 1996. In the Bible (Exodus 30 & 34), Moses was instructed to 'skillfully blend' spices together to make both the incense (symbolizing prayer) and Anointing Oil (symbolizing God's blessing). And so it is with the sincere incense of prayer that we offer these spices to you; every one of which has anointed our own marriage and family life with the oil of God's blessing.

## Using this Book

Try any of these methods to get the best flavour from reading 'Marriage Masala.'

- Find half an hour each week to sit down together and read a spice aloud. Using the 'spice it' suggestions, decide how you can put the ideas into practice.

- One or other of you individually pick a spice that fits your need or interest. Put it into practice and see if either of you notices the difference!

- Meet with some other couples, pick a relevant spice and use it as a launching pad for your discussion and share ideas for spicing your marriages.

- Give one away as a great wedding or anniversary present. (read it first before you wrap it up.)

# Contents

# Committed Forever

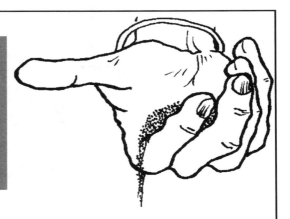

I heard a story once about an old couple that were celebrating their diamond wedding anniversary. Sixty years of marriage. After the special celebration the family had arranged, one of the great-grandchildren did his best to ask the old grandmother (who was very deaf) a question. 'Aggi, sixty years is a very long time. Have you ever thought of divorce during all those years?'
Aggi pondered for a minute, then she looked up at the young fellow, her wrinkled face gleaming and eyes twinkling as she replied, 'Divorce? Never. Murder? Several times!'

## Shutting the back door

*Our marriages are a mixture of good times and bad, laughter and tears. We are being unrealistic when we fail to recognise this. The most important word in our marriage is not 'love', 'sex' or 'happiness', but <u>commitment</u>.*

Gloria let the sand fall through her fingers as she contemplated my question. We were sitting together on a shady patch of sand in the mango grove at Cornerstone House. I had asked her, 'Do you want to shut the back door now, Gloria, and decide not to run away?' She had been contemplating escaping out of her marriage; running out of the 'back door'; away from the pain and having to work so hard at their relationship.

## It Happens and We Panic...

It doesn't take much to lose touch with each other. Sin, temperament differences, demands of work, children. It happens and we can panic. This is particularly true if we ourselves come from homes where out parents have separated or divorced. We can feel as if it we're inevitably heading for failure. A friend told me how, early in her marriage, her husband only had to gently criticise her, for her to feel full of terror that he would leave her and her small daughter, just as her own father had done years earlier. It was as she allowed God to move into her life and deal with the seedbed of fear and insecurity that she was able to trust her husband and choose to be committed forever to him, no matter what. Yes, it may take hard work, but it's worth it to close the back door as later Gloria chose to do. This isn't just starry-eyed romance,

*It was as she allowed God to move into her life and deal with the seedbed of fear and insecurity that she was able to trust her husband and choose to be committed forever to him, no matter what.*

steamy love-making, lingering walks down the beach hand in hand, honeymoon hugs and cuddles. It is, as it has been said, 'a definite refusal to give up'. So what helps us? What makes us able to shut the back door of escape?

## Some Ideas

Rod and I have found some practical ways to demonstrate commitment to each other through the rough times and the good:

- Pray fervently for one another. Not just about the problems, but for each other. Perhaps our greatest responsibility as wife or husband is to pray, to soak each other in prayer from head to toe.

- Choose to affirm and respect each other, especially in words.

- Decide to listen to each other, keep working at understanding.

- Have courage and talk about the tough stuff.

## The 'L' Plate Principle

This principle is the essence of commitment, the stuff of learning. One young couple decided to hang an 'L' plate on their bedroom wall. 'Every time things get tough, we can look at it and remember that we're learners and we'll make it!' As learners, we need to keep looking into the Trainer's Handbook (The Bible) for His instructions on how to love and live committed forever.

## Spice It Up
- Re-read your wedding vows together.

'I _____ , take you _____ as my lawful wedded husband / wife, to have and to hold, from this day forward, for better, for worse, for richer, for poorer, in sickness and in health, to love and to cherish until we are parted by death, and to this I give you my word'.

- Think of times when you have achieved, survived and weathered the storm together.

## Spice from the Word
*Hebrews 13 vs.4-6*

Notice how the writer of Hebrews emphasizes God's rock-like commitment to us, 'He himself has said 'I will never leave you, nor will I ever desert you'. He is totally committed to us, and here the writer emphasizes this wonderful truth in the context of sex, and money (verses 4-5). Take time together to consider the reliability of our God in these crucial areas of marriage. He holds out to us right now total security, stability and refuge.

# 'You're My Star'

*'Greet Auntie Anne.' We train our children constantly until they finally get the message. 'Say thank-you to Uncle Ashok for the chocolate', 'Don't rush past Mrs. Janob', 'If you knock into Roshim say 'excuse me' or 'I'm sorry'.'*

**When guests come into our homes we are extra attentive and thoughtful. India is known the world over for hospitality and generosity to visitors. Nothing is too much trouble. A meal prepared at any time of day or night for an unexpected guest is normal; the best bed is given to the visitor and careful attention to all they need to make sure they are well looked after.**

## Taking each other for granted

Somehow we often don't apply the same rules in our most important relationship. In the early days of our marriage we may. Husbands bring home a gift; compliment their wife on how beautiful she looks. She naturally enjoys the feeling of being treated as someone special and appreciates him and says so. What happens, though, to all this attentiveness and kindness, even good manners, after a few years of marriage? **We take each other for granted.**

Rajan has just got back from a church meeting, rushes into the bedroom to change. 'Coffee ready?' he calls, 'I could do with some'. No greeting, no eye contact, no touch or kiss or 'Have you had a good day?' from either of them. Sharon, busy with the children's homework, makes a coffee and puts it on the table. Without a thank you or even a look at Sharon he says, 'Oh, by the way love, I've invited the pastor for dinner with some foreign guests who are here for special meetings, hope there's a good meal ready'. Sharon walks back into the kitchen as Rajan flicks through the TV channels. Rajan and Sharon are not unhappy in their marriage but over the years they've begun to take each other for granted.

## Take Two

Now let's see Take two.

Rajan has just got back from a church meeting, arrives home tired, longing to relax and have a coffee. 'Hello, love' he says and squeezes Sharon's shoulders as she sits with Priya doing her homework, 'How's your day been?' 'OK, but we need to talk about whether I can manage working next Saturday. Would you like a coffee?' 'Yes, please'. Rajan joins Sharon in the kitchen as she makes the coffee, wraps his arms around her from behind as she stirs in the sugar. 'Um, that smells good, so do you, so does...' 'Hey, no time for that now' she laughs and teases him as she hands him the coffee cup. 'Thanks, love. Oh, by the way, the Pastor wanted to bring some foreign visitors here for a meal, I said I'd discuss it with you, shall we have them tomorrow night?'

'OK, I've got a half day too, so that will be fine.'

'Sharon, you're my star.' Rajan breathes in the peace of being home and takes a long sip of his coffee.

## A Special Look, a hug or a kiss

Often if one partner comes home and immediately rushes into some activity without even a greeting or greets another family member or guest first, ignoring husband or wife, this feels like rejection. It hurts and this thoughtlessness often results in missed opportunities to express our love and gladness in one another. After all, we wouldn't treat guests like this.

Do we still say 'Thank-you' or 'Do you think this will work?' or 'Would it be OK with you'. Phrases like this show our partner that we are aware of them as people with their own needs and not taking them, their time or care of us for granted. Do we still make a point of greeting each other when one has been out even if only for a few hours?

A special look, a hug or a kiss makes you feel great and you know that it's good to be together again.

Isn't our life partner the most important person? When they come home safely again after weaving through city traffic in the rush hour on a scooter, show them that you're glad they're safely home. We can't afford to take one another for granted. Give the extra look, remember to say 'hello', 'goodbye'. Recognise in a fresh way how important your partner is and demonstrate it by small details of thoughtfulness. He or she is your Star!

 **This week's Spice**

Read aloud together *1 Corinthians Ch13* in a translation' you don't usually use. Try putting your names in place of' 'love'. E.g. 'Love is not aggressive but courteous' (v.5).

 **Spice from the Word**
*Proverbs 18 vs.20-21*

Words are powerful! The Bible repeatedly warns and instructs about our words. Are your words being used to 'bless' or to 'curse' your loved one? Check out *Matthew 12 v.37* and *James 3 vs.6 & 8.*

# Praying Together

> I silently steamed! Not just because the night was hot and sticky and the power was off again, but because I was so angry with Rod. I can't even remember now what the reason for the anger was, but I was furious. We lay in bed, the dark clammy night hanging heavy around us.
>
> 'NO!' was my quick reply when Rod gingerly reached across to me and rubbed his foot on mine and said 'OK, shall we pray?' Pray?! Now! When I'm furious with him? 'You may', I growled. After a long pause he did. I began to cool down, my pressure cooker tendency, and reached across to give him a hug. 'I'm glad we prayed, we still have to talk about it though.' 'OK, now or tomorrow?' Rod replied, very tolerant of his 'do it now' wife.

***Another day, another choice. Often a hard one, to pray together DAILY; whatever the weather, whatever the time, not depending on our mood but daily.***

We have all heard the cliché 'the couple that prays together stays together'. There is maybe some degree of truth in this, although any couple that sees praying together as a type of marital magic is in for a shock! We need to be willing to invest ourselves into obeying all God's principles for a successful marriage and applying tools of wisdom in our relationship. Yet there is probably no better way of enriching our relationship and keeping God in the centre than deciding to spend time with Him together in prayer. Most couples accept this as an ideal but when it comes to practice they encounter all sorts of problems or excuses. This week we look at some of them.

But...

- **'We have family prayers with the children'**

  God has intended that the two of you become 'one flesh' and in this unique relationship praying together means often bringing areas of your lives, your hopes and fears for the future, your sex life, your disappointments and needs to the Lord. This openness is not always suited to family times of worship and prayer, good as they are.

- **'Because of our jobs we are often apart'**

  Decide on a time of day, say 1 p.m. (lunchtime) or 1 am, when - wherever you are in the world - you will pray for one another and then when you are at home together, pray together.

- **'Our way of praying is so different'**

  Good! God created variety! Tongues, weeping, laughter, methodical lists, written prayers, sitting, kneeling, long, short, however different your style of praying is, pray together.

- **'We can't keep it up. It lasts three to four days and then we stop'**

  Start again! Don't let guilt and failure discourage you. Forgetting to pray together or allowing it to slip out of your marriage for a while does not mean God loves you any less, but be sensitive to the Holy Spirit's prompting to start again. It will take effort and it may be just one of you that keeps remembering. Keep at it. The more you choose to make prayer part of your marriage, the more your marriage will become one of prayer.

- **'We can't fit it into our day'**

  We're being very unrealistic and setting unreasonable goals if we think we must spend hours together in prayer every day. For example Rod and I find that some days have been so hectic and full of time and people pressure that a sleepy 'thank you for each other' is all we can manage as we fall exhausted into bed. Try not to get stuck into a slavish system. The bottom line is simple. 'We will pray together daily'.

Perhaps this will be over the telephone while at work, driving the car or scooter, with eyes open(!), late at night in bed, a prayer walk together, sometimes a lengthy time of intercession planned ahead, a coffee break turned into a prayer time. Rod and I have decided that whatever the day is like, when we are together we will not go to sleep unless we've prayed together. Length of time, place or routine is not the main issue. If couples do have a routine lifestyle, then it is possible to have a regular time of day to pray together but still be flexible and adapt to changing family needs.

- **'I can't pray when I feel so angry, it's hypocritical'**

This excuse just digs us deeper into our rut of bitterness and hurt. It does take grit and determination, often with tears, to say, 'Let's pray', when it's the last thing we feel like doing. I'm very aware that I often wait in self-righteous silence for Rod to suggest we pray when I'm offended and hurting. As we choose to pray together it's a big step in the forgiving process. We sometimes say sorry vertically to the Lord more easily than horizontally to each other. Of course this needs to be followed by confessing our failure, hurt and pain and forgiving one another. We stand hand in hand under the spotlight of God's grace. Dare we say that there is anything in our marriage that is too big or hurtful for the grace of God to heal?

---

*We met Joshi and Pradeep again six months after they'd been attending a seminar at Cornerstone House. At the seminar Joshi had told me how distant she felt from Pradeep. She had honestly admitted that their sex life was 'hopeless', and she was struggling with outbursts of anger at her two-year-old. Basically she felt trapped in her marriage. Now six months on when I saw her she looked so different. 'Joshi, what's happened to you?' I asked. 'I can't remember much from the seminar, Ruthie', she told me honestly, 'but for the last few months we've started praying together every day. Sometimes just for a few seconds, other days for an hour. Our relationship is so different'. I could see it. She looked different, attractive and she'd even got a new hairstyle!*

---

**This week's Spice -
Look up Hebrews 4 vs. 14-16**
The choice is ours. In *Hebrews 4 v.16* we are encouraged to come boldly, together, to the throne of God, to approach him with the confidence that he understands our problems, sympathizes with our struggles and shame, and provides us with grace that is adequate to work through all our circumstances for His purposes and our blessing. If you already pray together, praise God. Keep at it... if not, start TODAY!

**Spice from the Word**

*Isaiah 30 v.18. and 45 v.19*

These two verses from Isaiah give invigorating spice for the times when we feel discouraged in prayer. God is ready to be found. If we seek Him He promises to listen. The God of compassion, love and forgiveness is there to rush and meet us.

# Leaving and Cleaving

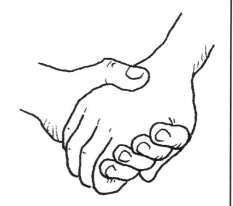

Two dynamic young couples visited us recently. Sam and Sheena, followed a couple of days later by Ravi and Rosie. Both have a passionate desire to discover God's plan for their lives together and serve Him. But sadly the similarity did not end there. Both couples were disillusioned; frustrated and angry, their tired eyes spoke volumes. Why?

> *... their tired eyes spoke volumes.*

As Sheena began to relax she confided about problems in their extended family. 'He's been beating me, it has happened seventeen times now. Although he is so sorry afterwards. He always takes his mother's side against me.' A problem with its roots in 'leaving'.

Ravi expressed his exasperation, 'Rosie always wants to be with her own family. I'll never match up with her brothers. She becomes alive there, but with me she's often so silent. I know we've only got a small house and it's sometimes tough for her, but she is always harking back to how good it was at her home. She's never satisfied.' A problem with 'cleaving'.

## Becoming One

*God brought Eve to Adam in covenant love and gave very clear steps for the success of their marriage. Genesis 2 v.34: 'for this cause a man shall leave his father and mother and shall cleave to his wife and the two shall become one flesh.* And the man and his wife were both naked and were not ashamed.' The very first instruction God gave for marriage was to leave father and mother in order to become one flesh. In real terms what does this mean to us?

> *... nothing should come between a husband and wife being ONE*

The underlying principle is that nothing should come between a husband and wife being ONE. This is a change in relationship from primarily being a son or daughter to primarily becoming a husband and wife. It is unwise therefore to keep depending on our parents after marriage although the Bible is equally clear that we are commanded to continue to 'honour our mother and father'.

## Is 'leaving' geographical?

In what specific ways are we commanded to leave and yet honour? Is it simply a geographical leaving? No. In some parts of the world, especially in an extended family, many couples will continue to live in the same household as their parents. There may be strong and valid reasons for doing so. This itself may not cause a problem if a clear emotional and psychological leaving or 'cutting the umbilical cord' has happened.

Time and again however, as in Sheena's case that cord between a husband and his mother has not been cut properly. He is primarily under the control of a strong manipulation. The warning sign to watch out for is when anyone is constantly coming between husband and wife, even though this may be with all good intentions or trying to help. They are being prevented from becoming 'one flesh'. This is clearly not God's intended pattern and therefore it may be necessary and wise to make a geographical move to leave the family home for emotional and psychological 'leaving' to take place. This may be a hard decision to make but it needs to be made if our oneness is under threat.

## Healthy Leaving and Cleaving

We appreciate the methods our friends Joel and Carolyn are working on to make 'leaving and cleaving' happen healthy for them. They live in an extended family with plans towards a geographical move later. They list several positive steps they have taken to make sure a healthy 'leaving' is taking place.

1. *Listen to advice from parents respectfully, but act on it only after agreeing together that it is correct for you as a couple.*

2. *Never criticise each other to our parents.*

3. *Give parents clear signals of our oneness by choosing to do things as a couple and creating our own unique family times.*

4. *Support each other at all times to our parents.*

**'You speak to her. How can we have a son-in-law who snores!'**

5. Demonstrate in words and practical ways our care and love for our parents and when moving away keep in touch with them regularly.

6. We should not be expecting their constant financial support: gifts are an extra blessing. Instead we should make sure that our parents' financial needs are being met, *1 Timothy 1 vs.4 & 8*.

## Get glued!

If thoughtful and thorough 'leaving' is happening then 'cleaving' should follow naturally. Literally 'to cleave' means to be glued or united together and to no one else.

Ravi's frustration was rooted in the way Rosie continued to have a focus on her own home and family roots and hadn't yet been willing to be 'glued to' him. As they worked on this together Rosie recognized that her primary relationship was to Ravi as his wife. Seeing their own uniqueness required her commitment and patience. It also required a conscious choice not to 'run home to mother' but actively communicate her needs to Ravi. This for Rosie meant sharing more and more of her innermost self with Ravi, allowing him into the secret places. Cleaving together through the good and tough times and not running away. She began to take seriously the words of *Proverbs 14 v.1*, 'a wise woman builds her house'.

### Spice for this Week

Are you 'glued together'? Look through Joel and Carolyn's check list and see if a healthy leaving with honouring is taking place in your marriage. Be honest and reach out for help if you need it, to follow this God-given command. It's often a help to talk through creative ideas of finding space for each other in an extended family, with other couples in the same 'boat'!

### Spice from the Word

*2 Corinthians 8 v.9*

Take hold of this verse today and consider what the Lord Jesus gave up or left behind to become your Saviour. Let your thoughts and meditation bring you to your knees in adoration of this mighty God who humbled himself, and didn't cling on to his rights or 'place for you'.

# Down to Talk

*Research tells us that on average, women speak something like 25,000 words per day! We cannot vouch for the authenticity of this research, but it sounds about right, doesn't it?*

It's often puzzling to a man how his wife can spend half-an-hour chatting to her neighbor on the phone, then meet her for a coffee later that day and still talk endlessly. He on the other hand might talk to a friend for a few minutes to arrange a meeting, discuss an issue related to common interests, work or sport but rarely just to chat!

Research documented in the book by Anne and Bill Mair, 'Why Men Don't Iron', shows us that the male and female brains, and in particular the connectors to the verbal parts of their brains are different. Women have highly developed connectors between both sides of the brain (the left verbal side and the right spatial side), whereas men have more connectors within each side of the brain.

Putting it simply, when a woman talks, she is using both sides of her brain drawing on wide in-built connections between ideas, emotions, sight, smells, the lot. When a man talks, he uses only the left side of his brain cutting out many

'You speak to her. How can we have a son-in-law who snores!'

other stimulants, and so tends to be more precise, or pedantic. A man does not easily verbalise his emotions but often processes thought through actions.

As husband and wife we need to be comfortable communicating in many different ways. This rich communication is a specific gift given uniquely to human beings made in God's image, reflecting how much he wants to communicate with us.

It's helpful to understand the four key levels of verbal communication:

## Level 1 - Hi and Bye

At this level, personal interaction is at its lowest. We pass like ships in the night recognizing one another, exchanging the time of day and maybe a comment on the weather, the train service or the government. But no response is expected or even wanted. Many women can't cope with the impersonality of this level and need to stop and visit the next level, even if just briefly.

## Level 2 - Passing of Information

Here we expect a small level of interaction. At its most basic: 'Pass the chutney' 'Ugh? Oh...' and he passes it. Most often we exchange facts and information that will affect the logistics of our day.

'Can you pick up Johnny after school today as I have the women's prayer meeting?'

'Ok, but can you buy bread on your way home?'

In a more developed way it can constitute the vast bulk of communication we practise between ourselves. We talk about our work, our relatives, our children, as long as we avoid words which give clues to how we are feeling about these matters, not really getting beneath the skin.

## Level 3 - Expressing Feelings

At this level some of us get uncomfortable because it involves emotions and opinion. For example, sharing information about the children's schooling is one thing, but showing a feeling that they are not doing as well as they should be, is another, and it immediately suggests an opinion, why I feel they are not doing well. An opinion may be critical or blaming. And blame has to be yours, not mine! If it's mine, I have to defend myself or find someone else to blame. So I may think, 'That's going to cause upset and anger. I can't cope with that, so let's avoid it. Better not to express my feelings in the first place. Better go up a level and stay at the passing information stage'.

> *Sadly many marriages retreat to level two and stay there.*

Sadly many marriages retreat to level two and stay there. They dare not raise their feelings, as one gets angry and the other upset, and they have not developed a way to progress. If this is suggestive of your marriage, then you will find the 'Listening to Understand' spice very helpful.

## Level 4 - Total Transparency

This is a level of communication unique to marriage. It is that Garden of Eden sense of being 'totally naked and with no shame', Genesis 2 v.24. We are not expected to be transparent to anyone else, not even to our parents or best friend, only our marriage partner and God, and that is why the Lord chooses to compare our marriage to His relationship with the Church, Ephesians 5.

Take time out to share your feelings together. Don't blame or take blame. Don't try and sort them or fix them, just share them and listen. Accept them, pray over them and ask the Holy Spirit for the power not to be enslaved by them. Do this for one another. Each day share a new feeling about a different area in your life. You will be a lot closer to really knowing each other transparently!

### Spice it together- 'Fifteen-A-Side'

Sit comfortably, relax and choose to listen to one another for half-an-hour. One of you begins and for fifteen minutes talks about whatever is on his/her mind without interruptions or questions. After fifteen minutes, exactly, on the dot or after fifteen minutes exactly, swap over. It's surprising how much deeper your communication will become.

### Spice from the Word
*Song of Songs 5 vs.2-8*

Reflected in these verses is a gradual, subconscious drifting apart into a state of self-occupation. Has that happened in your relationship with God or with each other? Is He knocking on your door and not getting an answer? Self-centredness can be the cause of communication problems with each other and with your Father God. The opposite of love is not hate but indifference.

# Make a Date/Time for Each Other

The other day we were asked; what in our opinion was the main problem couples had? That's hard! But without breaking any confidences we could say that from amongst the couples we knew, much of it centred around their willingness to give time to each other. ***To give time means we care, our wife/husband is high in our priorities. Not to give time communicates that we don't care, or possibly that we have pushed our partner down in our level of time priorities.***

## Spice Time

The fact that you are taking an hour each week to work through these spices is, in itself, making time for each other! Better still plan now how you are going to be able to give more and more time to each other as the years go by.

## Write your own names into your diary

A few years ago, Ruthie and I started to plan into our diaries 'R2' time (Rod and Ruthie time). We plan this time well in advance, write it on the calendar and make sure nothing else edges it out. When we worked up in Mahabalipuram, at Cornerstone House, Ruthie would come into Chennai very early in the morning to meet me off an early train when I would have been travelling. We went to a small hotel near the station and would have a leisurely breakfast together. The staff at the hotel know us well now, and always ensure we

'What is the problem love? I've arranged to see you between the bank manager's visit at 5:00p.m. and my dental appointment at 5:15p.m.'

have a quiet corner table! Or it may be an evening out for a couple of hours.

Occasionally we are able to get a full afternoon or even a full day together, when we will take a picnic and travel to a quiet shady spot, where we know we can be uninterrupted. Sometimes we will have a specific agenda, like preparing for a seminar coming up, or listening to each other on a particular 'burning issue' (see spice on Listening to Understand) or planning our schedule for the next few months. Other times there will be no specific matter and we will just catch up with one another.

## Ruling the Pressure

For many of us it is not the lack of wanting time together, it is just for lack of making time. Our lives are ruled by work, travel and school schedules which get more and more demanding as the months go by.

Jesus said 'Take my yoke… my burden is light'. But often our yoke is rock-heavy! Does this mean that we often take on more than we should and forget to ask our Father for His orders?

**Not the lack of wanting time together, it is just for lack of making time.**

We know that city life especially in a hot or humid climate can drain every ounce of energy from us, and it is as much as we can do to get through the necessities of every day, not to mention having any extra time for each other. We drop into bed exhausted and wake up knowing that we have just had enough sleep and any gift of free time is an opportunity to sleep some morel If this is true of your life, something has got to give somewhere and you are going to have to do some serious thinking about your lifestyle (see spice on Time Management). So despite all the other pressures, **you decide together to give more time to one another**. How and when?

## Change my attitude

Firstly, change your attitude towards you partner!

Apart from our God, our wives or husbands are the most important asset in our lives. Yet some of us treat our wives as if they were just a piece of moveable furniture, a cupboard to dump in dirty clothes and take out clean ones, or a vending machine which gives a monthly allowance and produces meals at set intervals.

Others of us treat our husbands like the number 53 bus. It arrives at 6.30 in the evening (usually late), spends the evening in the depot in a semi-stupor and being fuelled, brushed down and spruced up, then leaves at 8am the next morning. Who would want to give time to a piece of furniture or a passing bus? No one. Take a new look at each other, our lives are short and each day of our marriage is a gift.

## Plan Time

Secondly, plan time. Take down the calendar and mark in dates when you will find time for each other. It need not be more than half-an-hour or an hour, if your schedules are very tight, but treat the date as seriously as you would a job interview. Nothing else will have precedence. Remind each other the day before. Plan the rest of the day around this time. Get excited about it! If your boss or a friend asks you for that time say clearly 'I'm sorry, I have another appointment.'

## The date is important

Thirdly, make the date important. Let your partner see that you feel it is important. Make sure you are not late for it. If there is an important matter to talk about over the time, tell each other and agree on it. Don't suddenly spring a 'heavy' on your partner. He or she will find ways of avoiding the next date!

## Unplanned Surprises

Fourthly, be quick to catch the times which are not planned. The sudden surprise holiday, even the illness that

**Whose quiet hour?**

keeps one of you at home, or the sudden arrival of a relative which gives you a free baby-sitter, make the most of it.

## Catch the Minutes

Fifthly, be creative and inventive in finding these extra few opportunities to be together. Can you find ways of travelling on the same bus to work? What about fifteen minutes doing a chore together in the kitchen? Walk home together from Church? Catch the minutes instead of waiting for the hours.

 **Spice it Together this week**
Get down that calendar. Take time now to look over the next three months and book in several dates together. Invest time into your marriage, it's worth it.

Read together this paraphrase of *Psalm 23* and let it speak into your busy lives.

### Psalm 23: A Japanese Version

The Lord is my pace-setter; I shall not rush!

He makes me stop for quiet intervals.

He provides me with images of stillness

which restore my serenity.

He leads me in ways of efficiency

His guidance is peace!

Even though I have a great many things

to accomplish each day,

I will not fret for His presence is here!

His timelessness, his all-importance

will keep me in balance.

He prepares refreshment and renewal

In the midst of my activity by anointing my mind

with his oils of tranquillity.

My cup of joyous energy overflows!

Truly harmony and effectiveness

shall be the fruits of my hours

for I shall walk in the pace of my Lord;

And dwell in his house, forever!

---

 ## Spice from the Word
*Proverbs 5 vs.18-19*

Romance is one of the most vital ingredients of a vibrant marriage. One of the ways in which we keep 'the romance alive' is by making a date for each other.

It is God's command for us in our marriages that we are captivated with delight by our love for one another; see *Proverbs 5 vs.18-19*.

# Make Your Home a Palace

Take a few moments to let your eye look around your home. I doubt if you will be looking at a palace! Many of us live in rented accommodation and for some of us who are newly married, we live in a room of our parents' rented accommodation. We seem a very long way off from our palace.

*We'd like to suggest that you don't need to marry a prince or be a celebrity to be able to live in your own wonderful palace just where you are. You just need a bit of imagination, creative thinking and minimal expense.* Remember God isn't honoured by shabbiness, neither is he impressed by poverty. He enjoys beauty and He made the world like that. Reflect your Creator in your surroundings. Here are some ideas:

## Some practical suggestions

Start with one room. If it's the only room you have, all the easier! But start with the room in which you spend the most of your time - the living room. These are just ideas to show you how simple it can be.

Paint three of the walls white or light cream. Use cheap distemper but if you can afford it, use an oil-based distemper. Choose a strong but not garish color to paint the fourth wall, preferably the wall opposite the most light. Choose some cheap rice-straw mats to use on the floor.

Make furniture; keep it as low as possible. Trunks or boxes covered with a sheet or bed cover on which you can put a couple of cushions make

**Make me a princess first**

ideal sofas. Long narrow mattresses on the floor can make excellent couches. Cut the legs of your old chairs down to 6 inches and paint them the same strong color as the fourth wall. Do the same for a small table. There's your dining area!

Use dry bricks and planks to make bookcases. If you want to fix them, use eight parts of sand to one part of cement. This will easily chip off later when you move house. Go to your local sawmill and buy some cut off logs. They make ideal low stools. If you purchase furniture, go to the second hand furniture places and purchase low stools or folding chairs which are not expensive but are interesting. You can also make low platforms 3'6' x 2'6' and 6' high and make mattresses to match. Two of these platforms put together will make a bed for guests. Four of them will make a double bed for you when your in-laws come to visit and use your bedroom. You can add one cane chair.

Add a long length of electric wire to a light hanging from the ceiling. By screwing hooks into the ceiling over the place you want a low light, you can re-arrange your lighting. Keep it low with wide shades. Try adapting objects. We have used the hats as light shades. Use table lights and wall lights - avoid tube lights as much as possible.

Add a few pot plants. Terra-cotta pots that have been painted can look very effective.

Clean the windows and keep the glass clean. Paint the frames.

Choose colors that match the strong color of the fourth wall and use contrasting shades of dark and light shades of that same color in your cushions and covers.

Hang pictures or wall hangings on the wall. Keep them low down and make a design with the way you hang them. Use the dominant color of the wall again either to match or contrast.

Have fun as an interior designer. Be courageous. Be bold. Your aim is to make anyone who walks in say, 'Wow - what a palace you have made!'

## A Haven For You Both

The spice this week is a very practical one, but is really important and can affect so many other areas of our lives. When we walk into 'our space', 'our home' that feels 'like a palace', it can instantly change our mood. It makes us feel special and it makes our home feel like a place of rest, a haven for you and your spouse, and that is a wonderful thing, it's good for us.

We may often feel we have to be austere and feel bad about being concerned with our surroundings, but Jesus enjoyed beauty. Remember the woman who poured oil over Jesus? People were shocked at the expense, but Jesus wasn't. He was touched by her knowledge of how special He was and how she wanted to show this. By making our home 'special', we show each other how important our partner is to us, and that is something God wants for us in our marriages.

It doesn't have to be over-the-top expense at all, but don't feel wrong if you spend a little time and money doing it. It's important - to your spouse, to you, and to God.

Remember again that God isn't impressed by dirty, drab homes - neither is he honoured by poverty. He wants us to enjoy creatively what he has given us, and share it openly with others.

 ## Spice It Up This Week

Go for it!

 ## Spice from the Word
### *Song of Songs 1 vs. 12-17*

Most of the woodwork in Solomon's temple and palace was cedar and fir. A cedar tree is tall, stately and strong. Does this image describe your home; it may be small but is it 'secure'? A dwelling fit for your partner and your Lord?

# Anger

*'Oh no, not the chapter on anger this week, it'll just tell us what a rotten couple we are - always getting angry!'*

## Creative and powerful

But wait - surprisingly anger can be a creative, powerful emotion to bring about what is right and good in the world. It is our anger in the world that drives change. Slavery, bonded labour, bride burning, child abuse; we should, we must, burn with anger for action against such things.

We are angry with ▬▬▬▬▬▬ our children if they tell a lie or touch an ▬▬▬▬▬▬ iron when it is hot. Our anger protects. *It is our anger in the* We are angry when a government official *world that drives change.* refuses to pass our papers without a ▬▬▬▬▬▬ bribe. Our anger stands against corruption. We seethe when the boss mistreats a colleague. Our anger works for justice. So what then is the problem?

> In the Bible God expresses anger and wrath. Jesus, in strong, righteous anger, threw over the moneychangers' tables around the temple. In fact we are told to be angry. Ephesians 4 v.26 says clearly 'Be angry but don't sin.'

It is how we express anger in our relationships which is often destructive. The reason is that although anger may start from a righteous base, it very quickly becomes unrighteous. I may start feeling righteously angry at my husband's thoughtlessness in using up the last bit of the shampoo when he knew there were more in the family to take a bath. But very soon my anger becomes directed towards the fact that I won't look my best without shampoo to wash MY hair; 'I'll pay him back by putting twice the amount of mustard in his sandwich tomorrow'. My two seconds of righteous anger became two hours of sinful anger! So how can I tell the difference?

## What is righteous anger?

### Unselfish

It is directed towards the suffering of others not of myself. There is a thin line between the two; for example, it is out of righteous anger that I will punish my child for telling a lie, because I want her to be a truthful person. However lurking at the back of my action could be the thought 'what will the other people think of me as a parent if my child tells lies?' If I allow such a thought to come to the front of my mind, as it will so easily do, my anger will become unrighteous and will burn with remarks like 'I don't want to have a child who tells lies', 'I am ashamed of you as my daughter.' This anger has become selfish, diverted to defending myself as a parent rather than helping my daughter tell the truth.

### Controlled

How often our anger flares out of control! We say things we do not mean to, we do things we would never do otherwise, we lose control and we lose our temper. We are far more likely to lose control when the person with whom we are angry is emotionally involved with us. So our children, husband or wife often are the brunt of uncontrolled anger. Anger can be more easily controlled when it involves people outside our emotional attachments, but within our family, especially with our partners, anger almost always will be uncontrolled.

**Chillies in the Tiffin**

To be uncontrolled does not just mean making a huge scene, shouting or slamming doors. Our anger can be as silent as death, and show very little outward sign, but can be equally uncontrolled in our thoughts about the person. We can murder a person in our thought life, when uncontrolled anger takes over.

### Directed towards the problem not the person

The amazing thing about God's anger with my sin is that he does not reject me as his child, even though he has had to bring the sin to my notice so that I deal with it. The consequences of my sin may cause me to think he has rejected me, but he never has. *Psalm 89 vs.30-34* gives us the truth, 'I will punish... but I will not take my love from him.' A while back we met a couple where the husband was frequently talking about his wife as untidy and disorganised. She felt demeaned and devalued as a person. His anger was directed at her and not at the specific problem of untidiness. Such anger can never build up a person, but always destroys them.

### Resolution, not revenge

Think back to the last time you were angry with your husband and wife.

How did you pay them back? Did you withdraw your love; turn your back when they wanted to make love? Did you grudgingly put food in front of him, or deliberately forget to buy her medicines? Did you silently sulk or refuse to pray with her?

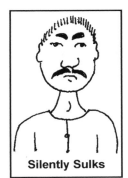

**Silently Sulks**

## Ask 'why am I angry?'

One of the most helpful ways to break the vicious cycle of unrighteous anger is to ask ourselves loudly and clearly-WHY?

Why am I so angry?
Why did I react like I did?
Why am I expressing my feelings like this?
Let the Holy Spirit convict us and show us a new reaction to the situation.

There is a way of escape from the patterns we are often repeating.

## Spice it this week

Make a list together of the things that have made you angry this week. <u>Think why?</u> Is it time to let go of the anger and ask for forgiveness? Is there some creative action to take which is inspired by the Holy Spirit and will turn the anger into a positive force for change?

## Spice from the Word
*James 1 vs.19-20*

Anger can build up so easily. Someone once said, 'Anger, the easiest thing to get, the hardest thing to get rid of.' James knew this and urged his readers to be 'slow to anger but quick to hear;' often that's the key.

We need to listen to each other more and ask the Holy Spirit for that fruit of self-control so that we will be slow to anger.

Notice in verse 20 how it says that 'man's anger does not bring about the righteous life that God requires' (NIV). Unrighteous anger gets in the way of our relationship with God and in turn other people - if we allow it. That's why God doesn't want it in our lives.

# A Garden of Spices

*Add water, wait for one minute and stir. Instant noodles, instant tea or coffee and ready mix cake. These days we expect everything to happen instantly. Life for our grandparents took a lot longer. There was time to pause, slow down and learn. Today, especially in urban life and with social networking, we increasingly expect everything to happen instantly; instant answers to all our questions, instant cures for all our ills, instant satisfaction in our jobs and instant responses from each other.*

*In fact this attitude filters into every part of our lives and expectations, even our sex lives. We tend to think, 'Have sex, instantly it should be great.' Making love however is an art. It's a skill to be learnt over the years of exploring one another's deep love, to discover the increasing pleasure of merging our bodies, fitting together as 'one body'.*

## High priority to the whole relationship

We need to recapture the atmosphere of the bride and groom in Song of Songs. The bride invites the groom to her 'garden of spices' to explore and discover all the delicious and tempting tastes and flavours. Nothing can be hurried. To her then, and to most wives now, love-making is an inseparable part of the whole relationship with her husband, and is an expression of warmth and affection. Someone said, 'If a man wants a good half an hour at night, he must watch the other twenty three and a half.' 'Instant sex' is not on the menu.

This is particularly important for husbands to understand because a man can easily separate his relationship with his wife from his sexual desires. He can be angry and rude and not say sorry, yet can be quickly aroused when he sees her undressing. But for his wife, she can't bring herself to make love if the last words with her husband were angry and hurtful. Perhaps what a friend of ours says is true, 'a woman's greatest sex organ is her heart.'

## Love-making is an all day affair

Gentle fondling in the privacy of the bedroom early on in the day, a whispered, 'you look beautiful', a tender look, some time to talk when coming in from work and shared children or baby care all help to build the sense of being loved as a whole person and improve our sex life.

**Lovemaking starts at breakfast**

Love-making is an all day, every day affair. We lead .our lover into our garden of spices not just for a quick 'nibble and run'. A loving husband will take the trouble to discover what his wife really enjoys and finds stimulating. Talk while you make love, expressing pleasure and excitement. Sometimes sounds may be more expressive than words! However wives need not, should not, be just a passive partner, waiting for husbands to take the initiative. Start practising the amazing art of seduction on your husband. Maybe a long lingering kiss or a certain perfume is just what is needed.

Variety is the spice of love-making too. It's important to be sure of privacy but try to be imaginative and find new places. Discover ways of making love in any part of the house! Try the shower, standing up, the couch, a chair, sitting in his lap. The possibilities are endless, exciting and fun to discover together.

### Don't forget to lock the door and pull the curtains.

If we focus on how best to please our partner and allow them to taste our 'spices', we shall receive increasing enjoyment, pleasure and fun ourselves. Most men reach a climax during intercourse but women need time to reach that peak of delight. In this garden of spices, foreplay is 'playtime' together, arousing one another to full entry. Start with slow and silk-like caresses. Stroking and running your hands all over your partner's body.

Your hands need never be still. Hugging and smothering one another with kisses on every part of the body, lead one another's hands to parts of the body you find exotic. Express the pleasure and excitement, getting timing right so that the wife is ready for her husband to come inside her. Above all remember that love-making is part of the whole relationship and the 'garden of spices' will thrive as friendship and trust bloom strongly.

**Spice for this week** Have fun practising and tasting the spice of your garden! Read together aloud, Song of Solomon 4 vs.12-16:

Dear lover and friend, you're a secret garden,
A private and pure fountain
Body and soul, you are paradise,
A whole orchard of succulent fruits
Ripe apricots and peaches,
Oranges and pears;
Nut trees and cinnamon,
And all scented woods;
Mint and lavender,
And all herbs aromatic;
A garden fountain, sparkling and splashing,
Fed by spring waters from the Lebanon mountains.

The Woman
Wake up, north wind
Get moving, south wind!
Breathe on my garden,
Fill the air with spice fragrance.
Oh! Let my lover into his garden!
Yes, let him eat the fine, ripe fruits.

The Man
I went to my garden, dear friend, best lover!
Breathed the sweet fragrance,
I ate the fruit and honey,
I drank the nectar and wine.
Celebrate with me, friends!
Raise your glasses - 'To wife! To love!'

(The Message *translation*)

## Spice from the Word
*2 Corinthians 2 vs. 14-15*

We all carry with us an aroma, not of actual perfume but a distinct fragrance of atmosphere. Paul talks about us being the aroma of Christ. In what ways are we the aroma of Christ to one another, our children and our neighbors?

# Boundaries

*Years ago I visited Pilani University in Rajasthan, India. I have a lasting memory of standing on the wall. On one side of the wall I looked at the barren sandy desert stretching for miles. On the other side of the wall were the lush green gardens of the university, with its peacocks, deer and even an artificial river. The contrast was unbelievable; it was a boundary wall that marked the difference.*

This must have been something of what was in the memory of Old Testament people like Nehemiah, Isaiah and Jeremiah when they bemoaned the fact that the walls of Jerusalem were all broken down. Without the separation, bandits and wild animals were allowed to plunder or pillage their beautiful city as they wished.

## Mutually agreed limits

When we talk about boundaries for a marriage we are not talking about rules and regulations. Instead we are talking about mutually agreed limits beyond which both of us agree not to go. You set these boundaries at times when you are both emotionally quiet and stable (like now), so that you can be checked by the boundaries when emotions and feelings run high.

## Keeping words 'safe'

Early in our marriage, Ruthie and I decided that we would never use the word 'divorce' in any confrontation we have. This has become a boundary for us. The fact that we have the boundary means that neither of us can shout divorce at each other in the heat of anger, we are quietly checked by a boundary we have set up when we are both cool.

**The No No word**

## Keeping actions 'safe'

We also need to set boundaries around our actions. For example, one may be that neither of us will walk away in the middle of a disagreement, leaving the matter hanging in the air. We added this boundary into one marriage when we saw how devastating this was for a wife we knew whose husband would constantly walk away. He would walk out of a room when he decided that he'd had enough! So they never resolved their disagreements.

## Teaching Children Boundaries

Tom and Tara had three little girls, beautiful, creative and lively children. When they came home from school there was bedlam. Their demands for snacks, entertainment, homework and tuition arrangements took up Tara's whole evening and attention. She believed this was the right thing to do as a good mother. Tom felt left out and unnecessary, longing for a good conversation with his wife, sharing the day with each other. He also wanted soma quality time with his children. They all needed to make some boundaries.

Boundaries are essential in the area of family life. We have tried to build these in as the children grow. One important one we have found very useful over the years has been a clear boundary of giving prior attention to one another before the children. This has meant teaching the children that when we are talking they wait before demanding our attention. It doesn't always work well, but having the boundary in there has meant we are less tempted to use the children as a buffer between us, as can happen if we are not communicating very well.

## 'Safe Space'

Boundaries can also keep us emotionally healthy. We enjoy having a constant stream of people staying, visiting or working In our home. We found however that we often had no time for each other, until a friend suggested that by closing one door and opening another, we could make our bedroom a place of privacy. We did this and are now reaping the benefits in our family. Our bedroom is for 'Gilberts' only! We can retreat there when we need to talk something over, or just be together.

A curtain dividing the room, a closed door or some cane chairs out on the terrace can all make 'safe space' for the family. Boundaries keep us in touch with each other.

## Spice for the Week

Draw a large square or hexagon on a sheet of paper. Imagine your marriage to be the space within those lines. Together write in the four to six boundaries you can agree on. Remember you must both agree on each.

Take your time if you find it difficult. Remember a boundary can be anything from words, phrases, actions, timings or physical arrangements, which will help you to build that wall around your 'garden'. You might like to involve your children in decisions for some of the boundaries if they are old enough.

## Spice from the Word
*James 1 vs.19-20*

When the beloved asks her lover to place her like a seal over his heart and arm, she is talking about protection and their unique oneness.

A married couple have a unity that no other relationship can have and this needs to be protected. One of the most important ways husband and wife can do this is by making sure they protect themselves by having mutually agreed boundaries in their lives. What are your boundaries? Do they give protection yet freedom to each other?

# Celebrations

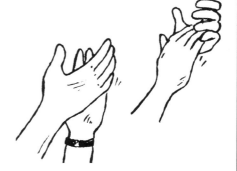

My family has some Jewish roots, which I deeply appreciate. Perhaps this is why the whole idea of celebration comes naturally to me. Jews delight in celebration! *All through the Bible, celebration is a strong element in God's pattern of things. So much of the Old Testament is full of praise celebrations, festivals and feasts. Their whole calendar was arranged around the celebrations of Harvest, Passover and Atonement.*

We can translate this type of celebration into our family and married life. Celebration is a way of reflecting God's delight in us, and in all he has made – seeing Him smile. It's a multifaceted precious diamond that we can use to bring sparkle into our lives together and, because celebration is something we do together, it brings us closer in touch with each other. This means taking every opportunity we can to celebrate! But how?

## Let's celebrate!

Planning times of celebration is a wonderful way of building up trust and security. Ways of saying 'I love you, you matter to me.' Birthdays can be a fun .way to start thinking of new ways to celebrate. In our family we have a tradition of a birthday breakfast with a red candle in a shining brass candlestick on the table.

We put flowers around the birthday person's plate and an exciting assortment of little parcels and cards. The birthday person has to stay out of sight until there's a loud chorus of 'Happy Birthday to you!' and then they march in as the start of the show.

It's variety and surprise that make it fun but also the feeling that 'this is my birthday and I'm special'; no matter how old you are!

In Rod's family his father's birthday was always celebrated with a picnic at the same spot each year. It was up a hill in a little clump of trees, where someone had once built a log hut. To celebrate in the same spot each year gave the family a sense of belonging and enjoyment of each other

## Babies, weddings, end of exams - any reason!

New arrivals, babies especially, exam success or completion of a difficult task, all give a wonderful reason to celebrate. Why do it? Just think for a minute of a family who have just heard of a baby's safe delivery or a couple out together for a wedding anniversary treat - what do you see? There's laughter and joy. A wonderful carefree jubilation that seems to add sparkle to their eyes and vitality to their bodies.

## Keep the wonder and delight

Celebration restores to us the childlike quality of enjoying sheer pleasure. I remember watching Ande and two small friends of his, leaping and dancing in the garden with a water hose. They laughed and rolled over and over in complete abandonment and delight as they splashed and sprayed one another. Sometimes we as adults can lose that wonder and delight in the gift of life and love together – all

'The wonder & delight in the gift of life…'

that our Father has given us. Jesus wants us to celebrate and be aware of His presence as we do, so that we recognise that he is Emmanuel – with us. What a wonderful guest Jesus was at the wedding of Canaan, producing the very best wine for everyone.

## 'The new wine of life'

In a very real sense, the new wine of life in all its fullness is a constant call to celebrate. Rejoice, rejoice is the trumpet call! The wonder of being redeemed, washed clean, forgiven and loved must be reflected in our delight in every day events and opportunities to give thanks to each other and to the Lord.

*When our daughter Prilla was eighteen, we recognized her special coming-of-age birthday and decided to celebrate. We began with a birthday breakfast, making sure the menu included Prilla's favorites. The day was full of surprises, hiring mopeds and taking a trip to a nearby river and water sports centre. Being a 'water baby' she loved this! We planned a surprise evening meal under* the stars at a local *hotel. We had lots* of fun, a night swim, *shared delicious* food and hilarious *memories together* such as 'Hey, do you *remember when I* sat on my cake at my *sixth birthday party* when we had a picnic *by Ooty lake?' Late that night, Prilla called me to her room and said 'Mum, I just want to say thanks, not just for today, but for everything. I really love you.' Prilla came into our family fourteen years ago as a little girl of four adopted from Mukti mission near Pune, India. With a sudden flashback to that day, tears of joy sprang into my eyes. That was the most precious moment of celebration for me, and I will treasure it always.*

**'Mum, I just want to say thanks, not just for today, but for everything.**

## Spice it up!

Find ways in which you can celebrate. Remember celebration is not only for birthdays and festivals. Try finding ways of celebrating:
- An Achievement - your husband mends that dripping tap
- A Milestone - you've lost 10 kg
- An Anniversary - 5 or 10 years in your house
- An Event - Moving to a new home

## Spice from the Word
*Revelation 19 vs.6-19: 21 vs.1-4*

The greatest celebration of all time will be the marriage of the Lamb. The King of Kings followed by the armies of heaven riding on white horses, dressed in fine linen (19 v. 14). He is victorious over sin and darkness (ch 19 v 15). This Royal rider is the Bridegroom of the church (21 vs.1-4). Reflect on the majesty, wonder, magnificence, and excitement of this glorious celebration. You are his Bride!

# Fruit and Root

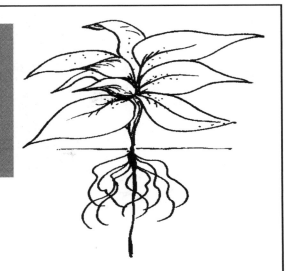

*I am looking out on a flourishing garden of coconut palms, mango trees, pink and white bougainvillea, flowering shrubs and bushes – such abundant luscious growth. The beauty is breathtaking, yet the secret strength of what I see before me lies below the ground - the roots digging deep into nourishing soil and water. Without these, the garden would dry up and die.*

## Roots and Resources

As individuals we need to recognise that our taproot, our deepest resource, is Jesus Himself and that He can truly meet our need of significance and security; that being 'in Christ' is being locked into His heart forever. To flourish in my marriage, my roots or resources must be strong and developing. In order to be the wife or husband God intended, my deep personal need of security and significance must be met.

## 'I need Jesus with skin on'

A while ago, I heard of a small boy calling his mother in the night. After getting up several times to his need of water, a sheet, the fan on, the- fan off etc, she said almost as a last resort, 'Rajan, you don't need anything else because Jesus is with you.' Rajan looked at his mother, big brown eyes open wide. 'Yes mum, but I need Jesus with skin on!' This is the greatest wonder of marriage, God has intended that we are Jesus 'with skin on' to one another to minister to one another's felt needs and to facilitate the meeting of those needs. So, how do we do this?

## What makes us flourish?

First we have to get to know what makes our husband or wife flourish - what are the roots they need for them to bloom best? Try this exercise for a bit of detective work!

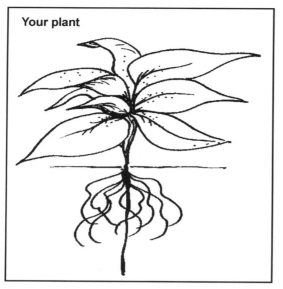

**Your plant**

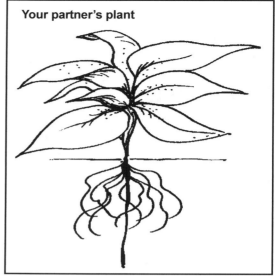

**Your partner's plant**

On the plant above ground, write in all of the gifts, abilities, qualities and vision that make you <u>uniquely *you*</u>. Do the same for your partner's plant. The taproot, which draws the main nutrients, is the relationship you have with Jesus though His Holy Spirit and God's word - that needs to be strong and healthy, see *John 15*. Now fill in all the subsidiary roots - needs and resources. Keep it simple. Be practical; for example, consider physical needs - sleep, sex, food. Consider emotional needs - time together without distractions, privacy. This will vary from person to person. Be creative and look honestly at first your own, and then your husband's / wife's 'plant'. Discuss what you have filled in to discover how you can help to meet these needs in each other. You may find out some new unexpressed needs.

## Manipulation is counter-productive

Most marriages are built on a demand to have our needs met first. Dr. Larry Crab describes this as a 'tick on a dog' relationship. *'The dilemma is that there are often two ticks and no dog!'* We become manipulative in order to get our needs met first. Manipulation is a type of deceit and we are all guilty of it at times. The underlying thinking is, 'Do what I want, when I want, or you'll be sorry.' Instead we need to admit our own needs honestly but focus on meeting our partner's needs.

## Take the manipulation test!
    a)   We usually go to the restaurant or visit friends <u>I prefer</u>.
    b)   I flare up in anger when he / she doesn't do what <u>I expect</u>.
    c)   <u>I joke</u> about his / her failures in front of friends.

d) <u>My attitude</u> is 'I helped you with that, now you must help me.'

Ouch!
I admit that all too often the 'meet my need' manipulative attitude creeps into my life.

---

 ## Spice for this week

See manipulation for the demanding counter-productive cycle of frustration it is, and with the Holy Spirit's power rid your life of it, taking *Philippians 2 v.3* as the spice for this week, 'Do nothing out of selfish ambition or conceit, in humility consider others as better than yourselves.' Choose some specific needs in your partner's 'plant', and decide to work at seeing that these needs are met.

'...**meeting each other's needs.**'

| | |
|---|---|
| A young mother, Lisa, with a six-month-old baby, often feels housebound and inadequate. One of her needs is to have time each week to meet a friend. Richard chooses to facilitate this need by making sure he comes home early each Wednesday to care for and spend time with the baby while Lisa meets her friend. | Tom is often stressed after the demands of the office - he would arrive home to be avalanched by children, visitors, news of the broken fridge, church meetings etc. To flourish as an effective husband and father, Tom needs quiet space alone to relocate his body and spirit to home. Anita chooses to facilitate this by giving him 20 minutes of uninterrupted space in their bedroom with a cup of tea to unwind with, as soon as he arrives home. |

---

## Spice from the Word
*Galatians 5 vs.22-23*

Read through that list of wonderful fruit which the Holy Spirit wants to produce in our lives. It's an amazing list, isn't it? God wants His people to live life in all its fullness, and the way He equips us to do this is by giving us His Holy Spirit. Pray and encourage each other through this list in Galatians this week, asking the Holy Spirit that through Him you both will produce fruit that enriches your marriage.

# Love Languages

When we first got married we lived in two very small rooms in the Indian city-Nasik. Rod in his eagerness to see his new bride settled and happy busied himself in building, fixing, mending and inventing new ways of making the best of the cheapest material. *I loved it all but how I longed to just hear him say, 'I love you.' When I asked him one day his reply was, 'But of course I love you! Look at all the things I'm doing for you'.* It took us time to understand that he was loving me in his own love language and I couldn't 'hear' it as it wasn't mine! All over the world, whatever the culture, love is expressed in five major ways:

## The five love languages

- Physical touch — of affection or acknowledgement
- Words of love — written or spoken; affirming
- Time — planned or spontaneous
- Gifts — thoughtful and relevant
- Acts of service — practical and caring

## Discovering Your Language

To discover your own love language, do a bit of detective work. Look at how you most enjoy expressing your love; five simple questions may help:

Physical Touch
Do you often give a touch to express love?

Words
Can you express your thoughts well in words, letters, a card, giving affirmation of your love?

Gifts
Do you love buying gifts and seeing the delight on the receiver's face as they open your present?

Quality Time

Do you enjoy lingering over a cup of coffee, being together or planning a surprise outing or booking a special date together?

Acts of service

How about working behind the scenes, making a needed cup of coffee, putting the special touches into someone's day?

You may find that all five are important to you; however one or two will certainly give you that 'buzz'. That is your primary love language. The way we express our love to friends, family and especially to our husbands or wives is the way we enjoy being loved as well.

Most of us have one major way in which we feel loved. For example, if you feel loved when you are given a gift, you will want to show or demonstrate love in a similar way. The problem is that your partner needs to receive love in their love language, which may be different from yours. What to do? Discover it!

Rod recognizes that **words of love** are very important to me. When we first discovered this, he found constantly repeating, 'I love you' rather monotonous! So instead of telling me, 'of course I love you', he chose to invent phases that were special to us, but meant those three important words, nobody knew what he meant, but I did and that made it all the more particular and intimate. *Proverbs 25 v.11* says, 'Like apples of gold in settings of silver are a word spoken in right circumstances.'

A friend of ours recently told us how he is learning to give his fiance 'killer compliments' **(words of love with encouragement)**. She loves it! Specific words of praise and encouragement meant just for her and nobody else. 'Your hands are so beautiful and they remind me constantly how caring you are.' 'When you said that your eyes were incredibly sparkling, I couldn't get enough of that look.'

If your partner's top love language is **physical touch**, it may not mean a strongly sexual touch but a kindness. Add a little variety to it, when he or she is reading the newspaper or working at home bent down, gently rub his or her neck. Think of it as a comforting act of tenderness. Put your arms around her, backed up with a feeling that says, 'I'm glad you are mine.'

**Gifts** may be very personal too. Flowers spell romance but so does an unexpected gift of your time, a phone call from the office at lunch time, a surprise outing at night, when everyone feels too tired to cook a meal at home. By speaking the love language of giving a gift, you are declaring

*'You matter to me, I have thought about you, I love you.'*

lovingly, 'You matter to me, I have thought about you, I love you.' It may be a way of saying, 'I'm sorry, please forgive me.'

Our marriage can become so businesslike. We can pour ourselves into our jobs, our children's education, serving and working in the church, extended family and community needs, so that gradually the ability to communicate love dies slowly, until we feel empty.

'Let's take the telephone off the hook.'

Time together may be what you are longing for. Booking into a diary a, lunch together; fifteen minutes walking together in the park in the evening; catching the minutes instead of the hours.

Be open minded, experiment, speak your love's top language as loudly as you can. Pray for creative ideas. Keep one another guessing as to what wonderful new ways of loving are coming around the corner. To some of us, a cup of coffee, just when we need it, the fan being fixed, the broken table leg mended, the bedroom repainted, speaks volumes. It says, 'You care about me, you love me.' If **acts of service** are your partner's top language, get to it now! The greatest enemy here is not lack of time to do these things, but laziness or procrastination. Do it today, this week!

##  Spice it together

Take time to find out your partner's love language. Without looking at each other's paper, write down the list of five love languages as they are listed above and put your own priority order, i.e. 1$^{st}$, 2$^{nd}$, 3$^{rd}$ etc. Now do it for your husband/wife. Try not to think too hard. Share together now, both of you, what order you have written. Surprised?! Often a partner is right about the top first love language but unaware about the order of the others. The key element here is to choose to speak in one another's love language as much as we can. To focus on expressing love in creative ways that means something special.

## Spice from the Word

Consider the ways Jesus demonstrated all five love languages. Here are some examples:
- *John 1 vs.42-47*, Jesus' encouraging WORDS to both *Peter (v.42)* and to *Nathaniel (v.47)*.
- *Matthew 8 v.3*, Jesus TOUCHED the leper, a sign of God's love.
- John 21 v.8, Jesus SERVED as he cooked breakfast for tired, sad disciples.
- *John 3 v.16*, Jesus GAVE everything for everyone.
- Mark 6 vs.31-32, Jesus lived out the principle of spending QUALITY TIME with those He loved.

# Honesty - The Best Policy

*1 John 1 v.7*, 'If we walk in the light as He is in the light, we have fellowship with one another, and the blood of Jesus, His son, purifies us all from sin.'

***Most of us would agree that being totally honest with each other is a good idea. Yet many people are afraid that being totally truthful is not helpful.*** In fact in certain circumstances they recommend dishonesty:

'How can I tell her that I might lose my job?'
'How can I tell her that I feel sexually useless?'
'What might he do if he knew about…? …it would be the end for us.'

It is true that dishonesty might be a short-term solution for peace. It may work for several months but in the long-term it lands us in a marriage built on lies. To avoid the fire we end up in the microwave!

## The Rule of Honesty

Here is a Rule of Honesty which we find helpful:

*I promise to reveal to you as much as I know about myself: my thoughts, feelings, habits, likes, dislikes, my post and present, my dreams and visions for the future.*

## Honestly expressing our needs.

'I promise…'

A marriage thrives on making adjustments to each other. We can't do this if we don't really know one another's true feelings.

Veena found her sexual relationship with Vikram more and more unfulfilling. He seemed to demand 'sex' without any romance, and her heart wasn't in it. Often she was tired after a long day and wanted to get to bed early. Vikram would stay up late and when he came to bed he would wake her up to make love. She could hardly bear it. She never told Vikram how she felt.

Some years into their marriage, while on a 'marriage weekend' away from their home, Veena sensed the Holy Spirit convicting her of her dishonesty. In other words she needed to gently but clearly express to Vikram how she felt, without condemning him, but honestly expressing her need. Vikram began to understand. He asked Veena to help him be more sensitive to her. He needed her to tell him how she felt so that he could make some adjustment.

## The truth will draw you closer

Historical honesty is tough. Honesty does not drive us apart. Dishonesty does. This is because often we need to lie continually to cover our tracks. It is the most precious gift in marriage to be known and loved and accepted for the person we truly are.

'psst, psst...'

Suppose you've had other relationships in the past, before marriage? What about some unfaithfulness now? 'I've lied to my husband about my past, how can I tell him now?' It may be hard, it may be painful, but the truth will draw you closer. No area of your life should be kept secret. All questions asked by your wife or husband should be answered fully and truthfully.

You may say 'If I tell her that she'll be devastated and never trust me again.' *Give one another the credit of being the most intimate person in your life and walk through the darkness of the revelation together, with Jesus who brings us into his light.*

*The right time is now*

*When even the most painful information is revealed, an opportunity for change, growth and forgiveness is given. This takes our marriage into a deeper level of intimacy than ever known before. Sometimes these revelations are best made in the presence of a counselor or trusted pastor to whom you choose to be accountable. When is the right time?*

*Now! Many of us wait too long, living under the fear of being found out. However we need to be caring and gentle in how we express things. If you decide to talk alone, choose a moment when you are relaxed with each other and have plenty of time. Then share it. Say something like, 'I've something to tell you, my love. It's not very easy to talk about but because I love you I must tell you and I don't want any secrets between us… '*

*It may be that you are at the receiving end of an honest confession. Allow love and respect to well up in your heart for your brave wife or husband. Reassure him/her that you love them, that his/her honesty deepens your love. Share also your hurt. Avoid the temptation to cross-question or ask for minute details. Allow your wife/ husband space and time to continue to be open with you.*

*You may feel emotionally 'kicked in the stomach' and having a trusted pastor or friend listen and pray with you is of great value as long as you are both in agreement about this.*

## Spice it together

Read through The Rule of Honesty together. Make the promises it encourages to each other and put it into practice together… now!

### A Warning:

Be careful that you don't build barriers to future honesty in your partner by saying things like, 'If you were ever to be unfaithful to me, I would never be able to forgive you and I would commit suicide.'

## Spice from the Word
*Psalm 48 vs.8-14*

God is totally honest with us. Transparency, where nothing is hidden, is God's ideal plan for marriage. Check out *Psalm 39 .vs.1-5* which again emphasises this pattern; the need to express ourselves and not to keep things hidden.

# Role-ing Together

Drop into a few homes around the city and meet some friends with us.

## Master: Slave

First we see a husband sprawled on his easy chair, a newspaper propped on his fat stomach, a cup of tea within easy reach. He takes a sip, makes a face and barks a command without turning his head. A little wife appears in the doorway. She takes the tea. He doesn't lift his eyes from the paper. She returns within seconds carefully spooning more sugar into the cup. She replaces it where it was and glides out. He ignores her, but when she is gone reaches out, takes a sip and smacks his lips appreciatively.

## My way: His way

In the second house we see a smart young wife on her mobile. She has her appointment diary open on the table and keeps glancing at the calendar as she talks. In an office several miles away, we see her husband on his phone, checking his e-mail. He is similarly looking from his appointment diary to the calendar. They mark dates and timings in their respective diaries, and then put down the phones. She snaps her phone into her handbag, and then straightens her hair in the mirror, gives some orders to the housemaid and glides out to a waiting taxi.

## Foreign Minister: Home Secretary

In the third home we see a harassed mother with three school-age children sitting at the dining room table. They are all meant to be doing their homework. She shuffles in her faded housecoat between each child and the kitchen, sometimes carrying the pot with her as she stands over a child helping them with their work. On one occasion, when she goes into the kitchen, the eldest child runs for the TV and switches it on, turning the volume right up. In another room the husband is packing his suitcase. He dresses himself calmly and smartly in front of the mirror. When he's ready to go he comes into the sitting room, thrusts a large wad of currency notes into his wife's hand, waves good-bye and leaves. She stuffs the notes into her housecoat pocket, slamming the pot down on the stove.

Which of these couples, if any, has got their roles sorted out? The Master: Slave concept has been a traditional one for generations. Perhaps in reaction to that, the My way: His way professional model has taken over. But when all options run out, most of us opt for a Foreign Minister: Home Secretary pattern. What is the Biblical pattern?

***As to be expected, the Bible does not describe one particular role pattern, but lays down various principles.*** Let's remind ourselves of them. It is important to set down firm foundations, so take some time to read *Genesis 1-3.*

***Back to Basics - Some key points to pin your thoughts on:***

a) **Man and woman have equal roles.** *Genesis 1 vs.27-31* makes it quite clear that man and woman were both given the role of 'ruling and subduing' the world together. Our society does not recognize this, because the curse in *Genesis 3 v.16* gave dominance to the man. If, however, we are to live in God's blessing, *Genesis 1 v.31,* we need to recognize that God created man and woman totally equal before Him.

'Equal' did you say?

### b) <u>**We have different responsibilities**</u>.

We are equal, yes, but we are different. Genesis 2 outlines our different roles. A quick summary shows that the husband's primary role centres on protection, value of work and activity with either his hands or his brain, *Genesis 2 v.15*.

He also has a major role in shouldering moral responsibility for the family, *Genesis 2 v.15*.

The wife's primary roles, on the other hand, centre around the joy of relationships, in friendship and companionship, whether in the family or out of it, *Genesis 2 v.18*. She also has the wonderful role of complement and helper. If you think these are inferior roles, remember that the Holy Spirit is a helper and a complement in what makes us whole! Yet again, the curse has ruined all this. The joy of work has been replaced by sweat and pain. The joy of relationships in the family has been replaced by drudgery, *Genesis 3 v.16*.

### c) <u>**Our roles are to reflect our Oneness**</u>. Every couple will decide differently how they work out the details of who does what in the home and family. Some will decide he makes the breakfast while she gets the children ready for school; others will do the opposite. Some will decide she will keep her professional job, while he changes his to suit the family and he works from home; others will do the opposite. Neither is more wrong or more right than the

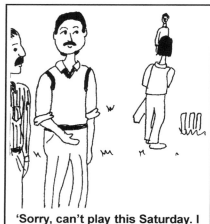

'Sorry, can't play this Saturday. I need to be at home while my wife is at her company conference.'

others. Yet all could be wrong if they are not mutually agreed on in an atmosphere of 'being one', *Genesis 2 vs.23-24*. The importance then is not what we do in our role, but whether we are working as one.

## What about our culture?

Patterns of behavior have been handed down to us. Some excellent models and treasures from past generations we need to value. Beware of 'throwing out the baby with the bath water'. However, all of our cultures must submit to the Word of God and His gift of freedom. Take another look at your family's cultural traditions in the light of this.

## Spice it

- This week consider whether you have been liberated from 'the curse' in the roles you have in your marriage. Read *Galatians 4 vs.3-5* (The Message)

> 'But when the time arrived that was set by God the Father, God sent His Son, born among us of a woman, born under the conditions of the law so that He might redeem those of us who have been kidnapped by the law. Thus we have been set free to experience our rightful heritage. You can tell for sure that you are now fully adopted as His own children because God sent the Spirit of His Son into our lives crying out 'Papa! Father!' Doesn't that privilege of intimate conversations with God make it plain that you are not a slave, but a child? And if you are a child, you are also an heir, with complete access to the inheritance.'

- List five of your own culturally dictated patterns.
- Talk over together how you would classify them in this table:

| Our family patterns | Freedom in Christ | Bondage | Not sure |
|---|---|---|---|
| 1 | | | |
| 2 | | | |
| 3 | | | |
| 4 | | | |
| 5 | | | |

## Spice from the Word
*Jeremiah 3 vs.6-10*

Frequently in the Bible those who rebel against God are referred to as being 'adulterers' (i.e. breaking the marriage vows). Jeremiah declares this. See also *Mark 8 v.38*; *James 4 v.4* and *Hosea 3 v.1*. Could there be cultural practises in our home that could be seen as 'adultery' in God's eyes?

# Time Management

Early in our marriage we lived in Panchgani, in the Western Ghats of Maharashtra in western India. I had two jobs: one working as a pastor in St Peter's Church, the second working as a youth evangelist with Scripture Union. During most weeks I travelled to either Pune or Bombay for three to four days on schools' missions. At home we had two hyperactive boys under five and a hyperactive dog. Ruthie ran a club for the boys at St Peters and together we were counselors for both the staff and the students. At the same time I was trying to write the teenage Bible reading notes for Scripture Union, running weekend camps at Nasrapur and building kayaks for adventure camps in the holidays!

'A hyperactive girl and a hyperactive boy and a hyperactive cat.'

We were young, Panchgani was beautiful and we enjoyed the busyness and variety. We were always on the go. It was toward the end of this time that a visiting friend suggested that I do a time and motion study. The idea was that at the end of each day, I would mark on pre-prepared graph paper the way I had used every fifteen-minute slot of my waking hours. I used different colors to mark in time working, eating, time preparing for ministry, time with the family, time travelling etc. It was a fascinating study, but to my horror it revealed that, over

**I was spending only about 2% of my time actually with my family, and all the time I was spending with Ruthie was virtually limited to sleep!**

a week, I was spending only about 2% of my time actually with my family, and all the time I was spending with Ruthie was virtually limited to sleep! We were both so busy that we hardly noticed the time we gave to each other. It was only the stark figures of percentages over the six-week period I did the study that made us aware of these subtle changes.

A short while later we were expecting our third child and we moved to Pune. One of the first things we scheduled in was a five o'clock walk along the paths and railway track near our home. The two boys would run ahead while Ruthie and I (with the third in a pushchair) would catch an essential hour with each other. But more than that, it taught us that you have to make time for each other, it won't come automatically.

Some people say it is quality time that matters, not quantity time. That's true, but in our experience, quality time only grows out of quantity time. You can't jump straight into two minutes of deep heart-to-heart intensive inter-action, if you are not spending ten times that amount of time .in the general chit-chat of just being together. But it takes discipline to get those twenty minutes.

## Making the most of time

There were many interesting things that emerged from my 'time and motion' study. I realized that I spent a good 20% of my time travelling. I began finding useful ways of using my travel time. In fact I learnt to sail while traveling between Panchgani and Mumbai. That is, I studied a detailed sailing manual on the bus! I also discovered that I was spending huge amounts of time in the bank or post office. I decided to pay a young man something extra to do that work for me. Then I also discovered that I was not spending enough time preparing for my ministry - part of the reason I was feeling so dissatisfied, as I was just repeating myself and going over the same talk again and again. I decided to give more time to preparation - and my interest and effectiveness in the ministry increased proportionately. This had noticeable spin-off in the quantity time and the quality of our family times.

'20% of my time travelling'

Jesus often withdrew to recharge, he sat and ate with his friends. Only a few meals are recorded but presumably Jesus ate every day and these times were probably times of rest and relaxation. Don't feel guilty about 'stopping times'. Jesus knew the importance of them.

**This week's Spice**

- Buy several sheets of graph paper and map out your week or do it on you i-phone. You may think you don't have time to do this, but if this chapter has rung bells with you then I seriously suggest you make the time to do this. You will reap the benefits, I promise.

- Each of you starts a 'Time and Motion' study for the next six weeks. At the end of each day take a few minutes to think back over the day and mark in your use of time. We suggest the following categories, but you will have to decide your own. NB: You have to be careful not to 'cook the books' by being dishonest! For example, be careful not to have three-hour quiet times during the six weeks, when you usually have three minutes!

  - <u>Just Living Time</u> (bathing, dressing, eating time)
  - <u>Quiet Time</u> (time you spend in prayer or Bible reading alone)
  - <u>Corporate Spiritual Time</u> (family prayer, Church, home-group etc)
  - <u>Work Time</u> (your paid employment or housewife time, or if you are in fulltime ministry - your direct ministry time)
  - <u>Personal Recreation Time</u> (time you relax - reading, watching TV etc)
  - <u>Family Time</u> (playing, talking, etc with the children or all-together times)
  - <u>Marriage Times</u> (time you spend solely with each other)
  - <u>Travel Time</u> (this may be family time if you use it to interact as a family, a personal recreational time if you use it to read a book. Or part of travel – mark it appropriately.)

- At the end of each week count up the minutes under each category and percentage them.

- At the end of the six-week period - study your percentages and make decisions about your time accordingly.

 **Spice from the Word**
*Song of Songs 2 vs.8-17*

The setting of this passage is the spring season. Here in the freshness, growth, vitality and aliveness of spring, two lovers are longing to spend time together, exploring and understanding one another. v.14 is a beautiful invitation from Jesus to you both. Are you willing to give Him time to enjoy His presence amongst everything urgent or important that presses in on you?

# Baggage Carrying

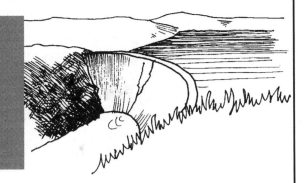

Recently we were working on a sketch for a seminar. It went something like this. Enter Joe and Reena. Each is carrying a smart leather case in one hand and an old plastic carrier bag in the other. For a long moment they embrace passionately. They come out of their kiss and admire each other's smart case.

**Joe tells Reena that his case is full of all the wonderful things he has for her during their life together. Reena replies that her case is full of everything she wants to share with Joe.** One by one all the objects in the smart cases are brought out and shown to the other who gazes rapturously at them. This is what is in each case.

<u>Joe</u>

All my love

My gentleness

My strength

My money

My Godliness

My lover's skill

My name

My sportsmanship

<u>Reena</u>

All my love

My tenderness

My persistence

My body

My compassion

My sexiness

My family

My creativity

After this exchange they continue to look lovingly at each other. They catch sight of the old plastic bags. Slowly, out come the contents.

**Joe**

My laziness

My fussy eating

My awful relatives

My smelly socks

My snoring

My insecurities

My early rising

**Reena**

My untidiness

My temper

My hours on the telephone

My nagging

My clothes buying

My painful memories

My late sleeping

## Coping with each other's carrier bags

*We are made male and female with all the uniqueness God intended but there's more to consider. Often it is the carrier bags we trip over especially when we are tired, or busy, or the children are sick or we generally feel low. Then we stub our toe emotionally painfully, on a piece of one partner's baggage.*

*So what do we do when the house is a mess and we want it to look tidy for visitors? Or clothes are left all over the floor for me to pick up yet again, meals are not on time or he watches endless cricket? Or she talks on the phone to a friend for half-an-hour yet again when the baby is crying?*

*This is when the nitty-gritty gritty of living together and coping with each other's 'carrier bags' makes' life difficult.*

## Taking Action and repairing the Wall

The problem is that these bits of our lives may seem to us unimportant. 'Why should she worry if I don't shave?' 'Why should he worry if I have six phone calls? Anyway, he's on the computer for hours.' The reason they are important is clear.

A repeated attitude partner that causes the a destructive chisel. It at love and respect in our behavior is habitual, grace we can have the

*It insidiously chips away at love and respect in our marriage.*

of behavior of one other to be unhappy is insidiously chips away our marriage. Most of which under God's power to change. Like a

crack in a dam wall, habits that annoy and irritate get more and more destructive, unless we take action and repair the wall. If we don't, all the water of love and respect eventually escapes.

## Name it and Change it!

Usually we are soft on ourselves and hard on our spouse when it comes to baggage. God commands us to 'look at the log in my own eye' first and allow Him to remove it. The first step, therefore, in clearing out the baggage is to acknowledge my own demanding habits and choose to change. Name it and change it! How?

1. Often the best way is to start by sitting together and writing down the habits you have that you know annoy your partner

2. Now change lists! Let your partner underline three that have the highest annoyance rate.

3. Begin to identify the reasons why they may be happening.

There may well be baggage that is very painful to deal with and a lot deeper than annoying habits. God longs, through his grace, to bring us to wholeness. If we let Him touch the habits in our lives, he can transform, renew and release us from them. Nothing is impossible with God.

Recently I was challenged to think through this issue again. As I read the list of the fruits of the Spirit in *Galatians 5* 'self-control' leapt out at me. I am not

'...writing down the habits...'

called, as a wife, to control or change Rod's annoying habits, just mine. It's so easy to become demanding or selfish in one's desire to see change in our partner. 'Do what I say, or else' is often a threat. Deep resentment or resignation follows this. 'OK, just this once', we say with reluctance - and so we have forced our will on to our partner. Dr. Harley in his book 'Love Busters' points out 'You can have a slave or a lover but not both.'

### This week's Spice

Don't be surprised if wives notice far more annoying habits than husbands do. This is quite common! Focus on three of yours ,you have both identified. Pray over them, however trivial they seem. Write them up on the mirror and accept God's grace to change. Help one another, pray specifically, but remember, especially wives, don't nag!

### Spice from the Word
*Song of Songs 8 vs.8-14*

Freely given love: the girl in verse 10 confidently moves from the past to the present in the joy and contentment of marriage. The joy of their marriage is the new life into which they are both now entwined. Throughout the song both lovers show beautifully how to give freely, to forgive, and to assume the responsibility for their own actions. Their struggles to give themselves freely knit them together in a deeper bond of love. This is the promise of God to us in our marriage as He leads us into the future and away from the past.

# And Baby Makes Three!

*At last that call came; it was his mother-in-law, 'Come as fast as you can, Priya is in labour; she's fine. The baby should be born by this evening.'*

Ashok was delighted. They'd waited several years for this. Both busy working together in their own flourishing software business, they'd decided to delay a few years before starting a family. But when the timing seemed right - nothing happened. As the months went by and curious aunts and grandmothers started up the questions, they began to worry. Priya felt depressed and dreaded the routine tests and hospital visits. Even their love-making seemed to have become set by the calendar.

But it all seemed worthwhile when eight months ago Priya had burst into Ashok's office, her face glowing. He had guessed right away! 'It's happening, yeah, I can't believe it, it's brilliant!' Priya was a bit embarrassed but nothing could wipe the grin off Ashok's face, made bigger when Johnny, his colleague, slapped him good-naturedly on the back, 'Hey, man! Made it at last, a dad-to-be, not bad!'

Now the time had come. As they lived in a remote place, Ashok had taken Priya to her mother's house six weeks earlier. Her family lived in a small town four hours away. Together they'd checked the local hospital and were happy with the clean, friendly atmosphere and efficiency of the young doctor. Now this call, should he take a day's leave? Yes, he would, he wanted to be there with Priya more than anything else. His baby, tonight, he could hardly believe it.

## Launched into Parenting

Pregnancy, babies; words that will change your life. How do you react? Jubilation? Shock? Excitement? All these emotions are felt plus lots more. You are going to be launched into parenthood; and baby makes three.

As we all know babies are deliciously sweet and cuddly, and a wonderful answer to prayer, but this is only half the story. Babies, and later children, are exhausting, demanding and seem to need our full time attention. It's amazing how one three kilogram infant can keep two or more adults busy twenty-four hours a day! Feeding, changing, bathing, rocking, cooing, playing, washing, stories, outings, school, discipline, homework, exams, studies, friends and so it goes on.

From the time our baby is first put into our arms until the day they get married, and even beyond then, they need us. They need our affirmation, security and unconditional love. Yet in giving it to them we must never sacrifice the primary reason for our marriage. God made us first to be 'one flesh' together. Secondary to that is to be fruitful and multiply, to have children and to look after them.

## Missing the pre-baby days

Ashok and Priya glowed with happiness. Their baby girl was born later that day. At first Priya stayed with her mother, and Ashok commuted. Two months later, Ashok brought her home to their apartment. They'd decided that Priya would stop work for a while to look after the baby. This was what they'd been waiting for.

A week or so after coming back home, they were exhausted. Ashok could hardly drive himself to work. The night hardly seemed to happen. The baby was up every two hours demanding something. As learners in the parenting game they weren't sure what she needed, a dry diaper, more milk, less covering, more covering?

She woke them anyway. When Ashok came home in the evening he would find Priya feeding, changing or holding the baby. All he got was a quick 'Hi'. He missed the 'old' Priya, the pre-baby days. At night Ashok loved to feel Priya's smooth, warm body beside him but when he tried to make love she shrugged him off, 'Not now, Ashok, I'm too tired.' Even when Priya's mother came to stay he felt rejected somehow. The women seemed to spend all their time fussing and cooing, feeding and bathing his daughter. For seven years, he and Priya had had one another and now, as much as he loved his little daughter, this baby seemed to have stolen his wife.

## Children can take the centre stage

Get the picture? At any stage or age our children can take top priority. They can become the main focus of our lives. We invest all our time, energy and love into them. God's pattern is different. His order for our family looks like this:

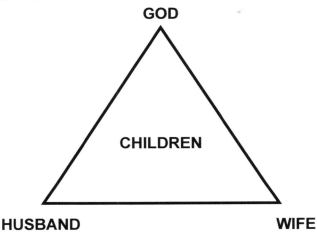

As we put God and each other into the right place the children are kept within the security of our unity and love. Consider how we can do this, especially when our children are very young, in the spice for this week.

## Spice of the week

The best gift we can give our baby is two united, loving parents. If your baby or children are calling the tune in your home, decide to work on some practical changes. This may cause a few days of a 'battle of wills' with your toddler, but in a few days' time you will ALL be winners.

The basic principle here is that we need to keep the uniqueness of our own relationship alive. Over the years we have observed several couples who do this well and some who don't.

## Helpful do's and don'ts

1. **Do** listen to advice but...
   ...**don't** forget it's your baby.

2. **Do** make discipline and baby routine decisions together and speak with 'one voice' but...
   ...**don't** forget that although it's only the woman that can breast-feed, a man can do every other job very well!

3. **Do** take time together away from the baby (or later children) for at least an hour a week and...
   ...**don't** refuse offers of help, baby-sitting or feel you always have to take the baby or child with you.

4. **Do** make sure that the baby does not come between you, especially in bed! So...
   ...**don't** forget that you begin the task of 'training a child in the way he should go' as soon as he/she is born. Train them in unselfishness.

5. **Do** enjoy, play with, talk to, laugh with your baby, but...
   ...**don't** rush immediately to every cry, demand or toddler squabble.

---

 ### Spice from the Word
*Song of Songs 7 vs.10-13*

These verses from Song of Songs chapter 7 remind us of the love a husband and wife should have for one another. The beloved and her lover delight in each other.

It is very easy in the busyness of family life, sleepless nights, early mornings, homework, mealtimes etc. to forget to nurture and protect your own marriage relationship.

Children need to see their parents expressing their love for each other. It's how they learn to express love later in life. It's not wrong for a husband and wife to show affection while their children are around or pay each other compliments.

Read through these verses again and' ask the Lord to show you ways in which you can appreciate your husband or wife more.

# Body Space

No matter how much we love each other sometimes we need time on our own. We can especially forget this if we are people-centred extroverts and thrive on company twenty-four hours a day! Picture us when we were newly married.

Rod says to Ruthie,   'I'm going for a walk'

Ruthie,                   'By yourself?'

Rod,                     'Yes, sometimes I enjoy being alone'

Ruthie,                   'Why? Have I upset you?'

Rod,                     'No, I just need a bit of space'

Ruthie,                   'Can't I come and enjoy the space with you?'

Rod,                     'Love, I need to be by myself'

Ruthie,                   'But I'm your wife'

Rod,                     'Yes, I love you, but I'm going by myself'

Ruthie,                   'I love you too and I want to come with you'

Rod,                     'No, really, I just need... sigh... OK, come if you like!'

Neither of us enjoyed the walk. I didn't because Rod was silent, striding out ahead while I got increasingly hot and cross, trying to keep up and wanting to talk or at least hold his hand! Gradually I've learnt and am learning that Rod really does need time on his own, more than I do, and that if I love him I must recognise that need.

## Time Alone

We need time alone for different things. Perhaps just to clear our heads, to get rid of that stress-headache, to process thoughts or to formulate plans and strategies. Sometimes we need a bit of body space from each other so that we can miss each other and fall in love again! If our homes are often full of people, friends and family dropping in, students coming in for a chat, hyperactive kids and a bouncy dog with a parrot thrown in, even the most extroverted of us will benefit from a bit of time alone.

## Spinning Plates in the Air

I began to feel the first stirrings of that need when our third son Dan was born. Luke was five and Ben was three. My life was full and I loved the hubbub and chatter of an overflowing house, yet at times it seemed I was constantly spinning plates in the air and if I missed the cue once the whole lot would crash round my ears. Above all I wasn't able to find any time alone for my own personal time with the Lord. There were just no margins of time in my life.

'half an hour with no other body too close'

Rod soon recognized the symptoms of needing a bit of body space and took over the 'before breakfast, and breakfast' slot and gave me half-an-hour or so of space with no other body too close by. It met my need.

## Peter and Serena

Serena has a full time job in childcare with her husband, Peter, who is a social worker. Their lives are full of administration, counseling and day-to-day needs of the children as well as their own bouncing three year old. Serena told me she never has time alone and aches for it. She longed to be able to do some embroidery, reading or writing a letter, alone.

Peter, being a 'people man', found it hard to understand what her problem was. He asked her to be specific about her need and she wrote it down. 'Three hours a week on my own and time on Wednesday evenings to shop or visit friends or perhaps go to the women's group.' They worked this out by rescheduling both their duties in the children's home.

Serena has taken up embroidery again. The spin-off is her enjoyment of Peter and her little boy for the rest of the hours in the week, which is making it worthwhile in Peter's estimation.

## Walking in Jesus' Steps

In our twenty-first century life it's difficult to find a place on our own and anyway are we just being selfish wanting it? No.

Jesus is our example. Look at the perpetual shouting, the pushing and shoving of people trying to touch Him, the heat, dust and sweat, the tiredness, the constant questions from his disciples, the teaching and healing, delivering from demons and battles with temptation. Jesus' life was packed full of people and their needs. He often had little sleep and hardly any time to eat. So Jesus took time off, alone, **to pray, to listen** to His Father, to be refreshed all by Himself. Picture Him trekking alone up a stony hill track, stopping half way up to rest, take a cool drink of water from a stream running down the mountainside; listening to the birds, watching the shadow of the clouds as they glided over the glistening water in the lake way below. Solitude. Jesus needed it and took it. So do we, if we are to walk in His steps. **Those of us who say we don't need time alone, probably need it the most.** 'Many people have not heard from themselves for a long, long time. Those of us who are always on the run never meet anyone anymore, not even themselves.' (Robert Banks, Tyranny of Time)

## Spice it this week

Plan one 'all on my own' activity each. That must mean that you are away from each other, the children, work, church, any appointments, the telephone and demands for at least three hours. Decide to keep it up for three hours a week for two months. At the end of that time assess what a difference it has made to you both. Release each other to find each other again!

## Spice from the Word
### Psalm 23 vs.1-3

Isn't it great that our God is the good Shepherd who longs to lead his faithful sheep to still waters?

This psalm is so familiar and so popular, maybe because the feelings we get when we read it are those of rest, peace and quiet. We all need those things and here the Bible backs that up.

Body space is important for all of us, husband and wife, and we need to make sure we are letting our spouse get the body space they need so they can be led beside 'still waters, to refresh their souls'.

# Listening to Understand

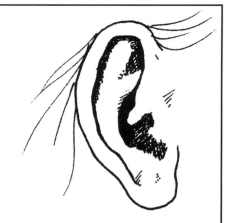

*If listening to each other were easy, there would not be over fifty commands in the Bible to 'listen' or to 'hear'!* The other day Ruthie needed to remind me gently of a habit of mine that was annoying the family. My immediate instinct would have been to jump to a conclusion as to what she was talking about, switch off from what she was saying and spend the next few seconds preparing my 'bullets' to refute, rationalise or defend myself. As a result, I of course would hear nothing of what Ruthie was really saying. So instead of just having a habit to change, I would now have created a partner to challenge!

## The Technique

However, several years ago, Ruthie and I learnt a technique of listening that has transformed our ability to cope with potentially explosive issues between us. It is called 'Listening to Understand' and it's extremely simple.

'A time & place alone'

First you need to choose a TIME when you are both free and when both of you have 'cooled off' from an emotional disturbance over the issue.

Then you need to decide on an uninterrupted PLACE together (maybe a snack and coffee in the corner table of a special restaurant or on the terrace after the kids are asleep). If you are busy people, book the time into your diaries and keep it like you would a dentist appointment! Pray together to begin with - just a simple prayer that God will enable you to listen to each other. And then in your special time and place one of you - (probably best to start with the least talkative. of you!) - starts to tell the other all that you feel about the particular problem. The other partner agrees to listen only. They must not interrupt but must keep giving the partner clear indications that they are listening - like looking at them, nodding, saying yes, or okay, or carry on etc.

After the first five minutes or so, or whatever is a natural break, the listening partner will repeat back to the speaking partner as much as they can of what they have heard, paying particular attention to what their partner has said about their feelings.

The speaking partner will then continue, clarifying any misheard statements. This partner continues for as long as they feel necessary until they know, from what their listening partner has repeated back to them, that they have been completely listened to and understood. It is important throughout to realize that this is not a discussion and the purpose is not to arrive at a decision or a conclusion about the problem. The purpose is solely to listen to understand what your partner feels about the problem. After the first partner has finished, it is now the turn of the second partner to speak all that they feel about the problem. Now the first partner seeks to listen and reflect back all they hear in just the same way. At the end of the time together, both of you should feel that the other has thoroughly heard and understood what you felt about the problem. You may not have come to any conclusion as to what to do, but by fully understanding what each feels about the issue, you have diffused the 'bomb' and gone well over halfway to making decisions that will work for both of you. It really does work.

> *Listening is the key to our ability to do what God wants of us.*

## Ears to hear but do not hear

*God's constant complaint about His people was that they wouldn't listen. 'Son of man, you are living among a rebellious people, they have eyes to see but do not see, ears to hear but do not hear', Ezekiel 12 v.2. Jesus, who was faced with the same problem, comments: 'This is why I speak in parables... though hearing, they do not hear or understand... but blessed are your ears (the ears of the disciples) because they hear. The one who hears the Word and understands it produces a hundred or sixty or thirty fold', Matthew 13 vs.13-23. The overwhelming thrust of Scripture is that listening is the key to our ability to do what God wants of us.*

*'My sheep hear my voice. I know them and they follow me', John 10 v.27. Quick to listen... 'the man who listens intently into the perfect law... not forgetting what he has heard, but doing it, will be blessed in what he does' - James 1 v.25.*

*A good listener to God can become a good listener to others. Meditate together on Isaiah 50 v.4. 'The Sovereign Lord has given me an instructed tongue to know the word that sustains the wary. He wakens me morning by morning, wakes my ear to listen like one being taught'. God knows what we need to function well as human beings and in our relationship with one another. He knows we need to be fed by Him and we do this by listening to His voice.*

## This week

Most of us will have what we call a 'burning issue' i.e. there is something which, if we try and talk about it, ends up in one of us mopping up tears and the other kicking the dog. Take time this week to listen to one another on the issue. If you think you might need practice, find a less explosive issue. Here are a few suggestions.

The way you drive

Our use of money

The TV programmes the children watch

Schooling decisions

Visiting those awkward relatives

## Spice from the Word
*Philippians 2 vs.5-8*

'Listening to Understand' builds a bridge to rebuild our communication. The supreme bridge builder is Jesus, whose love for us did not consider equality with God something to be grasped at but,

- made himself nothing

- took the nature of a servant

- became obedient to death

- even on a cross

Praise him! Is listening so hard?

# Pancakes

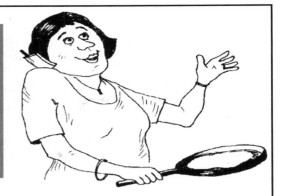

## Totally equal

We're different! 'Men are from Mars, Women are from Venus' says John Gray. Variety is the spice of life! A great deal of research and writing has been helpful in exploring and identifying male and female differences. However, there is a danger here. It is only a short step to move from saying 'we are different' to saying 'you are worse', 'not as good as' or 'below'.

**_God has created us equal. Totally equal; but excitingly different._**

Many of the small irritations and sadness in a marriage come from a failure to understand and appreciate our differences in a positive way. Let's look for example at the way that we think and process decisions differently.

## Excitingly different

A friend of ours in San Francisco, Tim, tells a brilliant story of a newly married couple. Imagine the couple at one of their first breakfasts. She has decided to cook pancakes. So, very lovingly she prepares the mix and the next morning excitedly presents the pancakes to her new husband. He licks his lips in anticipation and gobbles them down. She watches expectantly for his reaction.

'Wonderful - not quite as good as my mother's, but very good!'

Then he blows a quick kiss and hurries out to catch the train to work. His mind immediately switches from home mode to travel mode. Will he catch the 7.51 or if he takes the short cut across the railway lines could he just catch the 7.43 if it's a little late? He decides not to take the short cut in order to buy a newspaper. He catches the 7.51 and stands all the way thinking about his assignments.

Meanwhile, back home, she has cleared the table rather grumpily and dumped the dishes in the dishwasher. She is annoyed that he referred to his mother's pancakes - a woman well

'He didn't like my pancake.'

known for her brilliant culinary skills. She grabs her books for work and gets out the scooter. She kicks it angrily into life thinking, 'That ungrateful fellow, why didn't he like my special breakfast?!' She speeds off to work, expertly steering through the rush-hour crowds, thinking, 'He didn't like my pancakes!' Her work that day as a teacher is just as demanding as ever - no let up from the 30 children in her class. Running through every lesson is the refrain 'He didn't like my pancakes!' - not that anyone would have known it as she efficiently handled her class, joked with her colleagues, and showed off her wedding photographs to some of the senior girls. But each time the refrain returned 'He didn't like my pancakes', it increased in intensity. She would never be able to cook like this mother; he would not like the food she prepared; he would start eating out; he would meet someone else who cooked better pancakes; he would start going to her house, or back to his mother's home for better breakfasts; she was no good as his wife. By the time she got home that evening, she had already decided that she was a hopeless cook, useless as a wife and a total failure. Meanwhile, back in the office, the husband has breezed through his office work, successfully dealt with several clients, advised his clerk to get married fast - it was the best thing in the world, had a foul snack lunch from the office canteen as he was late, visited two retail outlets; popping into a shop on his way home to check the football scores, then rushed to catch the 5.10 train back home. As he squeezed into an impossible gap between a fat commuter and a student carrying a huge bag of books, he smiled to himself - anticipating the joy of coming home to his lovely new wife. He must buy her some of those cookies he knows she loves. He walks briskly home from the station - forgetting to buy the cookies in his eagerness to get home fast. He throws open the door shouting 'Hi Babe!' He hears a clatter from the

'What pancake?'

kitchen and finds his wife scrubbing the breakfast dishes. Coming in behind her, he puts his arms around her, and to his surprise she shrugs him off. 'What's wrong? Was the principal rude to you? Why are you crying? What has happened at school?' he questions. She blurts out - 'You didn't like my pancake!' Cries again. In complete amazement he says, 'What pancakes?'

I'll leave you to imagine what happened next! This story illustrates the different ways many men and women think.

## Men think in 'boxes'

A man often thinks in boxes. When he is at home, he thinks home, family, wife and children - just home. When he travels, he thinks in the travel box - how can I get there faster, I've got to overtake that fellow, how can I get a seat etc - just travel. When at work, he thinks just work. When with friends - he thinks just friends etc. Of course, this is a generalization but men's minds tend to be rational, logical and cope best with focussing on one thing at a time and maybe in great depth.

## Complementary

Because we our perspective is different, our of each other are our solutions to are different. answer is not change our thinking, but complement understanding so that we can 'perfectly one'.

Look at v5.22-23. We the glory of in spite of our we can continually more united and to one another.

### Women think in 'spirals'

A woman, on the other hand, has a mind that is more like a spiral than a box. She has a greater capacity to think about a wide range of issues all at the same time, not compartmentalizing them like a man. While fully involved in her demanding work, she can be thinking about her family, friends, shopping, the sermon last Sunday, what her husband said to her at the breakfast table and a host of other things. There may be' no obvious link between her range of thoughts, as she thinks more intuitively. She comfortably multi-tasks. Watch her before breakfast. A mobile phone tucked against her ear nestled into her shoulder; laughing with a friend as she talks animatedly about a plan to meet her for lunch; at the same time frying eggs at the stove; as well as bending over to do up four-year-old Johnny's shoe-laces while simultaneously tying ribbons into six year-old Tanya's plaits. No problem!

think differently, on the world expectations different and problems T h e to try to ways of to try to o u r of issues become

John 17 can reflect Jesus as, differences, b e c o m e complementary

## Spice it up

- Analyze how you both think. Generally men think more analytically and women more laterally. You may find it helpful to picture that in terms of a man thinking in depth and a woman thinking in width, both are necessary to cover the whole expanse. Of course, you may find that the wife thinks deep and the husband wide, or you both think deep. Don't worry, God hasn't made a mistake! You are unique as a couple.

- Select a non-emotionally charged issue in your lives together - a neutral area - and brainstorm together some new ways of dealing with this issue. For example, say a neutral area for you was 'travel to work'. (OK, I know for some of you it will be the one thing that almost makes you want to commit murder; in that case, don't choose it - yet!). Sit down with a large sheet of paper between you and each of you with a pen. Put down all you think. You'll be surprised at the creative ideas you could come up with of how to get to work!

- Now try this method of dealing with a more 'central' issue to your marriage. Appreciate each other's different perspectives on the issue. Grow to a better understanding - move on to some decision-making.

## Spice from the Word
*Genesis 12 vs.7-31*

Up to this point God had given a word of authority, 'Let there be light, ...Let the earth, or waters, produce...' but NOW with all the affection of a father, he says 'Let us make man.' Together with the Son and the Holy Spirit He plans a unique creature - a man and a woman - made in His image. Picture yourself walking with Him, together in the Garden, revel in His delight and what he has created.

# Decisions, Decisions

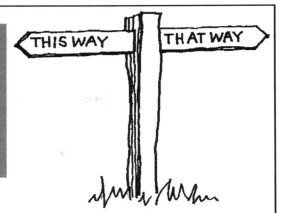

*When faced with decisions of any kind there are essentially only five possible answers, yes, no, wait and a mixture of ideas or new ideas! Unfortunately, there are a hundred thousand ways of getting to any of those five answers! Our problem is often not the answer at the end, it's getting to the end!*

We heard of a couple where the husband boasted, 'In our thirty years of marriage, we have never had a disagreement.' Our reaction to that statement was, 'Poor wife!' Decision making is a process that may cause greater conflict than anything else, yet it is a crucial skill affecting every area.

Whether it's:
- How we discipline the children
- Who does the washing up
- Which TV programme to watch
- When to visit the in-laws
- What to buy
- Or a major decision like:
  >> whether he should take the new offer of a job abroad
  >> or whether you should move to another place

All decisions demand attention to some basic principles.

## Made to be one

Togetherness: You are made to be one, made to pull together. So all decision making needs to reinforce this. Some couples function by allowing certain decisions to be made by one partner and others to be made by the other. For everyday decisions this is obviously a good you

## Made to be one

practical way in our busy lives, but where decisions involve <u>emotions</u>, we need to make them together.

Some decisions may appear calm and simple on the surface, like who washes the dishes after every meal, but below the surface may lurk ravaging sharks ready to turn the kitchen into a blood bath!

'That lazy lump, dumped in front of the TV while I slave away in here' or 'she makes me do women's work! I'll show her.'

So it is important we identify the decisions that stir deep feelings in either of us, and ensure that those decisions are made together.

## Listen first- then decide

Communicate: It stands to reason that the better the communication, the better our understanding and it should therefore follow that the better our understanding, the better our decision-making.

We have found in our important decision-making that we need to have at least one session of 'Listening to Understand' before we can even begin to make a decision. By doing this we give each other the chance to fully communicate our feelings about a particular decision, which enables us to understand where we stand in relation to the decision that has to be made.

## Map it out

Before Ruthie and I began the Cornerstone House Family Ministry we spent a weekend with an older couple who had much experience in counseling. One of the first things they did was to spread a huge sheet of cheap paper (like the paper used as tablecloths at weddings) on the floor. The four of us sat on the floor around this paper each armed with a felt pen. As we talked we scribbled all our ideas and thoughts down on this paper. As we saw it all mapped out in front of us, it became much easier for us to see how Cornerstone House should shape and how we and our large family fitted into its demands, problems and opportunities.

'That lazy lump...'

We made several crucial and lasting decisions while sitting on the floor in that small flat! Try it just the two of you, and if it is a major decision and appropriate, draw in other family members or close supportive friends into the mapping process.

## It's our decision

Owning the decisions, it is important that new decisions made can be 'owned' by both of you. It may be that in the process of decision making one of you will have to relinquish a pet idea. I well remember the last time Ruthie's nesting instinct began to ache for another chick in the nest. We already had four great kids and our youngest son Dan was then about eight. I'd been well and truly operated on making any natural addition an impossibility, or at the very least a miraculous act of God!

I began to process the decision making heavily loaded against any such thought. I thought I was too old; we already had four, (two more than the world population quota!) we had a lovely adopted daughter; we couldn't afford it; I was too busy, too tired, too anything. I had countless reasons as to why Ruthie had to be sensible and stop giving these sort of melting mother looks to every baby that passed!

Well as any husband will know, your wife may have no reasons, no logic or argument, except to say 'I just know we should', and eventually you realize that in matters like this she's, well, just right! To save face I probably went on reasoning for a couple of weeks, but I knew she was right. I needed to come to the point of owning that decision as the one I agreed God wanted us to make. Of course it was very shortly after that point when God brought Ande to us as a tiny scrap in a purple blanket, and it took no more than a couple of seconds of that little chap in my arms, to realize that I was going to be able to thoroughly own, and thoroughly enjoy the wonder of this precious life coming into our nest.

## Heads I win; tails you lose!

The question is often asked, 'What do you do when you just cannot decide?' Sometimes two options are so equally weighted that you cannot decide, or maybe neither one of you is able to relinquish your opposing point of view. It seems that every alternative is impossible. What do you do then?

The Biblical principle here is that the husband needs to prayerfully, responsibly and humbly take a decision for the family and ensure that all follow through on the consequences, however tough. He must take the responsibility for seeing the decision through, especially if the benefit of the decision takes a long time to reap. Be warned, this is not permission for dominant husbands to bulldoze their wives into quick or selfish decisions. Together we need to listen, brainstorm and accept wise advice from those who know us well, wait, pray and listen for God's answer. Only then can he take caring authority. Read *Ephesians 5 v.21*, before you read v.22! 'Yield to obey each other because you respect Christ.'

##  Spice for the week

Tackle your decision making with new energy! List down the decisions you have shied away from making. Put them in order of priority. Begin with the first, and proceed towards making the decision by:

1. Setting aside enough time for a 'Listening to Understand' on this area.

2. After listening fully to each other's feelings, sit down around a large sheet of paper and brainstorm, mapping the whole decision area. Record many of the feelings and facts that arose in your talking in the 'Listening to Understand'.

'Tackle new decision making with new energy!'

3. Pray over the result of the brainstorm and MAKE A DECISION.

4. Agree to own the decision together no matter what.

5. Act on it.

6. Review together the result of your decision.

## Spice from the Word
*Genesis 1 vs.26-28*

One of the first principles in creation is that in God's sight men and women are to work in equal partnership. This is God's wonderful 'big picture' plan and affects any decision we make. In v.28 'them' refers to both male and female being given commands and blessings together. We are a partnership making choices, discovering God's will and working for His glory. Keep the 'big picture' even in small decisions.

# Shake the Sheets

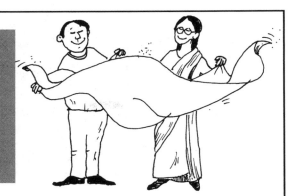

***The only disadvantage in living by the beach is that sand gets everywhere*** and into everything. It can rub our bodies, chafe our feet and irritate our eyes. It even gets into our bed! Now a few grains of sand can be handled ok, brushed off the sheets no problem, but when various family members' sandy feet and bodies have deposited more and more, there's nothing' for it but a good shake of the sheets to get rid of the sand or we won't get a wink of sleep.

## Sand that rubs and hurts

The rubs, chafes and irritation in our marriages are a bit like that sand. Tiny grains of hurt which cause most of the problems. A wife feels hurt because her husband forgot their anniversary, or criticized her mother. A husband feels hurt because his wife doesn't understand his work pressure or insulted him in front of his friend.

Basically being hurt is our response to disappointment or offence. Then we keep thinking over how we've been offended and allow one hurt to pile up on another; just like accumulated sand in the bed. We have a problem because accumulated hurt leads to angry attacks and hostility and we are allowing the little grains of sand to pile up into skin, chaffing pain.

## The union of two forgivers

This pain will not go away if hurts are denied or kept hidden inside. We need to 'shake the sheets' and be forgiven, small offences that each other so *learn to forgive and be forgiven,* and learn to forgive especially for the can rub and chafe easily.

'You didn't notice that I've tidied the house so thoroughly.'

'Didn't I? I'm sorry, please forgive me.'

'Hey I wish you wouldn't interrupt me when I'm talking, you kept doing it when we were at the Raos' house, and it really embarrasses me.'

'I'm sorry, I'm afraid I just suddenly think of something and blurt it out. Please forgive me.'

Robert Quillen, writing about marriage, said 'marriage is starting to love over and over again; a happy marriage is the union of two good forgivers.'

Shaking the sheets effectively also means that we learn how to express our hurts, desires and frustrations honestly. Most of us don't. We just give hints and off-hand comments.

Richard says, 'Wives should be submissive'

Richard thinks, You hurt me when you shout at me in front of the children

Anita says, 'Husbands should be more respectful of their wives' schedules'

Anita thinks, I was upset because you didn't call me to tell me you would be late.

It is much easier for us to make a vague accusation about respect or submission rather than deal with our disappointment honestly and concretely, admitting we are upset because of a husband who didn't phone to say he was going to be late, or a wife who shouts in front of the children.

## 'I feel' statements

*Hurts are about feelings. Remember the sand, it rubs. So make 'I feel' statements to each other, rather than accusations. Compare these statements and see the difference:*

'You don't know how to handle money' or 'I feel frustrated about our finances, can we talk about how to keep to our budget?'

'You are so insensitive' or 'You probably didn't mean to hurt me this morning but let me tell you what it felt like to me.'

Just like the sand isn't always in the sheets, so we need to keep our communication about our hurts true. It's easy to exaggerate, 'You always come home late', 'You never help me'. We need to be realistic, truthful and accurate.

## Shaking the Sheet Together

It takes two to shake a bedsheet! Don't avoid doing it by walking away either literally or emotionally. The accumulated grains of sand or hurt may cause so much anger that we take the easy way out to avoid conflict, to escape. Our pride or wounded ego causes us either to shout, slam a door, leave the room or burst into tears and sulk. Just try to picture this scene.

- Husband comes home late
- Wife shouts
- Husband blasts wife
- Husband leaves room
- Slamming of doors
- Wife cries
- Sulky, silent dinner

Following a process for shaking the sheets, getting rid of accumulated sand is a great help. Try this one:

1. Arrow prayer for self-control, an essential fruit of the Spirit

2. Admit my own feelings and express them constructively

3. Speak out words of forgiveness and repentance, 'I'm sorry, please forgive me', 'I forgive you.'

4. Decide to be solution centred (see spice on Making Decisions)

## Spice it up

Is there 'sand in the sheets' in your relationship? Are you angry, bitter and hurt about the little things? Discuss it if you can. If that is hard write a letter expressing your love yet also mentioning specific hurts. Are you guilty of hurting your partner? Confess it, express real sorrow and ask for forgiveness. 'Shake the sheets' together.

## Spice from the Word
### Hebrews 3 vs.12-14

Reflect on this passage together. There are three key words to respond to. Watch your HEART (v12) and repent of any HARDNESS (v13), HOLD FAST to faith in the Lord Jesus. Encourage one another to take these commands seriously.

# 'I am the Boss!'

*'Ahh - this is the spice I've been waiting for. My wife has been getting a bit too bossy; I need to put her in her place!'*

## 'I am the Boss?!'

Well Husbands, let's see how you can achieve this according to the Bible! Does the Bible appoint us as 'the Boss'? The husband is definitely referred to as 'The Head', see *Ephesians 5 v.23: 1 Corinthians 11 v.3*, and he is referred to as the one who 'rules over his wife', *Genesis 3 v.16*, and the one

to whom his wife 'submits', *Ephesians 5 v.22; Colossians 3 v.18; Titus 2 v.5* and *1 Peter 3 v.1*. For many of us husbands, that is enough for us to d e c l a re unquestionably – 'There you are, I told you so - even the Bible agrees with me. I am the boss' – and we ensure that our wives and family have no doubt about it. But is this God's Biblical plan? Take a closer look.

## Jesus liberates from the curse

Firstly - the reference to 'ruling our wives' in *Genesis 3 v.16* is actually part of the curse on mankind. It is not something God originally ordained for us. In fact, it's what Jesus came to liberate us from, *Galatians 3 vs.13-14*! And anyway, even if we were permitted to 'rule over our wives', the way we rule would have to be as Jesus ordained in his instructions to his disciples,

'Not as the Gentiles who lord over them... instead whoever wants to become great among you must first be your servant' (*Luke 22 vs.24-26*).

Headship for the husband in the Bible is defined always in comparison to Christ, our head of the church. Nowhere is Christ referred to as the 'boss' or 'ruler' of the church. He is 'Ruler over the nations', *Romans 15 v.12*, but 'Head of the church', *Ephesians 5 v.23*; *Colossians 1 v.18*. And as a Head, His relationship with the church is exactly opposite to being a ruler or boss! It is described in *Ephesians 5 v.25* as 'love for the church' and 'sacrifice for the church'.

**Headship for the husband in the Bible is defined always in comparison to Christ,**

So husbands - here is the first shock for us men! If I am going to act as a head for my wife, I am going to put away all ideas of being 'the boss', and realize that I need to act like Christ to the church in my attitude to my wife - that is in love and sacrifice for her.

## To sacrifice my life for her

Read again carefully verse 23 of *Ephesians 5*. 'For the husband is the head of his wife as Christ is the head of the church of which he is Saviour'. It is so clear that the way we are head is 'as Christ'. It is further defined in verse 25, 'husbands love your wives, just as Christ loved the church and gave himself up for her'. The astounding teaching here is that I, as a true head of my family, am to be prepared to lovingly sacrifice all that I value most for the sake of my wife. It even suggests that I am to be prepared to sacrifice my life for her.

That looks OK in theory. Maybe we would nobly declare that yes, we would definitely defend our wives and families against any thief or murderer who attacked them and yes, we certainly would throw ourselves in front of them to protect them from a charging bull or elephant. Unfortunately, the Bible is not really talking about murderers and elephants here; it's talking about:

- Sacrificing time... like when I want to watch sports and she wants me to accompany her to buy a pair of shoes

- Sacrificing relaxing in the comfortable chair with that cold drink - to putting my wife in the comfortable chair with the cold drink I make for her

- Sacrificing going to meet my parents, to accompanying her to visit her brother, whom I find so irritating!

Christ is intensely practical in the way in which He loves and serves us as His church - His bride. His door is open; His supply is extravagant; His time is everlasting; His joy is exuberant; His forgiveness is ever ready. Take a few moments now, husbands, to confess your lack of Christ-likeness in love and sacrifice for your wife.

## Spice it this week

Husbands : Consider and write down two specific ways in which you can demonstrate loving sacrifice for your wife, and then do them!

Wives : See if you can spot your husband's efforts, and reward him appropriately!

## Spice from the Word
*Colossians 1 vs. 16-17 & 19*

There is one amazing characteristic of Jesus that is overwhelming: humility. Just for five minutes talk through together what He gave up to be your saviour. Now read again these verses. The 'greatest ever', the creator of the universe doesn't become 'Boss' but took the form of a servant, died a martyr's death and yet triumphantly rose again with all of Heaven shouting out His glory and His greatness. Husbands, what a supreme pattern to follow!

# You are promoted!

**Husbands - if you thought that last week's subject was hard enough - wait for this guys!** *Ephesians 5* has more to teach us about headship, and it's all hard stuff for husbands!

Drop into a very typical home. Well-educated husband and wife, two children, one mother-in-law, eight fish in a tank, a cat, a car in the yard below and a leaking drain. The wife works part-time to supplement the family income. The husband comes home late one day to find that the wife has crashed the car; the children have fed the fish to the cat and the mother-in-law has slipped on the water leaking from the drain. How does the husband react? A typical reaction (not yours, I'm sure) would be to crack the children's heads together, kick the cat, scream at his wife and pack his mother-in-law off in a taxi to go and see the doctor.

He then proceeds to lay down the law for his children, forbidding them to go within ten feet of the fish-tank; and forbids his wife from driving the car in the future as she is obviously incompetent with poor eyesight, just like her mother (why else would she slip on the drain water?). The repairs will definitely come out of her salary, not his. Having sorted everybody out (the cat escaped out the window), he self-righteously slumps down in front of the TV to watch the news.

A typical husband? A little exaggerated perhaps, but yes, two very typical attitudes came through. One - I'm the law giver and I make the rules for the rest of my family to obey; and two - I'm more capable than my wife and I need to organise

her within her limits. Ephesians 5 has some very challenging things to say to these two attitudes:

## Grace livers or law givers?

Firstly – we are not law givers; we are grace livers. Verse 26 talks about Christ cleansing the church through the washing of water of the Word. Cleansing in the Old Testament was through the law – but cleansing in the New Testament, and now, is through grace. Grace is not something we can reduce to rules, it has to be experienced and lived out. Grace is soaking love in the empowering presence of God to enable us to be what He wants us to be; and to do what He wants us to do.

Law is easy. It can forbid the children from going within ten feet of the fishtank. Grace is more difficult. It begins with understanding. Perhaps by understanding the frustrations of two active children cooped up in small apartment, with a father who comes in late. It then teaches repentance and forgiveness. Perhaps by the husband's apology for failing to fix the drain - an apology that the children would see and hear as he arranges to take his mother-in-law to the doctor. If I, as a husband, am to be head of my family, I need to demonstrate God's cleansing in grace, by showing and asking forgiveness which means often having to say sorry to my wife and even my children. Forget about emphasizing law and start living grace.

---

### Promote my wife

Look at *Ephesians 5 v.27* again and consider the amazing way in which Christ as Head of the church prepares her to be His glorious bride in Heaven. For many years I could never see the relevance of this verse to my headship in marriage. But I now understand it as being crucial

*to promote... so that her gifts and abilities come to full expression.*

– that Christ wants me as head to promote Ruthie so that her gifts and abilities come to full expression.

Yet how often the opposite is true, where a husband will feel threatened by his wife's abilities and will try to 'keep her in her place' or speak disapprovingly of his wife, even in front of the children. Some wives in a mistaken understanding of submission will actually want to take such a position, and allow their children, especially their sons, to take pre-eminence over her. The Bible's teaching will never allow a wife to take such a lowly position. She is a bride of glory and it is our duty, husbands, to ensure she grows into that position.

 **Spice it together**

### Focus on the bride!

- Talk through together her God-given gifts, talents, interests and dreams.
- Try together to fill in the chart for her:

| My talents and gifts are: | My interests are: |
|---|---|
| | |
| **My dreams and ambitions are:** | **Most of my time is spent on:** |
| | |

- Brainstorm to see how she can grow in the expressing of her full gifting and ability. Think about areas, where, for whatever reason, she has not been able to express her full gifting or ability. How can you both let that gift be promoted?

- Read *Colossians 1 vs.9-10* and let this truth under gird your decisions.

**Spice from the Word**
*Matthew 6 vs.25-34*

Famous words, but still absolutely true… 'All these things will be given to you.' Reflect together on these verses. What have you both 'set' your hearts on?

# Submission – a Loaded Word

'Submitting yourselves one to another in the fear of Christ, the wives to their husbands as to the Lord because the husband is the head of the wife as Christ is the head of the Church and is Himself Saviour of the body. But as the church is subject to Christ, so also should wives be to Christ in everything... Let the wife make sure she respects her husband', *Ephesians 5 vs.21-24 & 33.*

**So there it is in black and white. We can't run away from it, wives!**

To submit to our husbands is right there in the Bible. One husband said to us recently when looking at the responsibility of headship, 'Wow, this is incredible; but it's all one-way traffic!' He is putting her first in sacrificial love, caring for her every need, promoting her, he is even her saviour. So now the 'traffic' moves the other way and of course, as a wife, I should submit to such sacrificial love just as the church does to Christ.

## Submission - a loaded word

Unfortunately submission is a very loaded word for us wives. Why? Because it's been loaded with behavior patterns that are recommended for wives in the name of being a submissive wife, but patterns that are actually rubbish! What picture comes to mind now of a submissive wife? If you're very honest it is probably an orthodox, quiet, domestic and quite honestly rather boring woman! What a shame. Let's clear away all the rubbish and then look at what submission really is.

## Load 1: 'Submission means I'm weak'

Wrong! Look at some Biblical patterns of submission. Elijah to God, Paul to Christ, Christ to His Father, they were totally submitted but they were courageous, clear minded, original thinkers and strong.

## Load 2: 'Submission means I'm silent'

Wrong! In *1 Corinthians 14 v.34*, Paul says, 'Get talking to your husband.' Communicate, communicate! Obviously this is not a license to moan, grumble and complain. If you hate spending time with your demanding sister-in-law, tell your husband. If you don't like his nose stuck in the newspaper at breakfast, express that. If he is being inconsistent with the kids, talk it through, honestly and lovingly.

## Load 3: 'Submission means I do all the domestic jobs'

Wrong again! Submission is not a 'job', it's an attitude of heart. I may keep a beautiful house, give up my job, cook the meals, wash the floors, change the diapers, be a terrific housewife but not be submissive in the Biblical sense at all.

## Load 4: 'Submission means blind obedience'

Sorry but no! If your husband is doing something that is without question wrong or destructive, then as his wife you should not obey that. Veena's husband, though a well-known pastor, regularly beats their children mercilessly without any sign of repentance. This is absolutely wrong, *Ephesians 6 v.4*. The children are in danger. Veena would be right to move away from him for a period of time to protect their children.

Christians are mistaken to insist that a submissive wife remain in a home where she is being physically beaten, or where the husband is being repeatedly unfaithful, violent or is mentally unstable. A period in a 'safe house' would be right under the care and support of Christian friends and family to bring about change and real repentance. Our obedience must be to God first. Think of Ananias and Sapphira in *Acts 5 v.10*.

> *Submission is not a 'job', it's an attitude of heart.*

## Load 5: 'I'm showing submission by covering my head in worship and by insisting my husband always runs family devotions'

Wrong again! Because the emphasis is on outward show. Head covering is not the issue here. It may very well be appropriate and correct in our culture but a submissive wife will, under her husband's headship, use her God-given gifts and abilities. Before she was married, in her student days, Sarah had a wonderful gift in leading worship.

Sensitive to the Holy Spirit, she led people in opening up to God in adoration and praise. For years after her marriage, this gift lay dormant because she waited for Thomas, her husband to lead. Tom couldn't get a note in tune and never opened his mouth in times of singing. The day came when he almost had to force Sarah to use her talent and not go on waiting for a miracle on his vocal cords! As he has 'promoted' her in his headship, this has given Sarah a new release as a submissive yet free wife, soaring in her spirit and strengthening the body of Christ and her own family. Tom said later, 'I'm the launching pad and she's the rocket!'

## Spice it this week

Look together at the pattern of submission you have adopted in your relationship. Does it carry a 'load of rubbish' with it? Check through each load and challenge yourself about a change. Prepare for next week!

## Spice from the Word
### *Song of Songs 2 vs.1-7*

Verse 4 - what does this picture mean to you? All attention is focused on this great banner. A wife needs to live in the supreme confidence that she is continually under the banner of her husband's love and care. The banner is on public display. He treats her both in public and in private with unwavering love.

# Set on my Feet!

*Having cleared away some of the 'rubbish' about submission, let's look at it again.*

- *It does not mean that I am a silent, subjugated slave of my husband.*
- *It's not a job, or role I take.*

## What is it then?

The secret is in Ephesians 5 v.22; 'Wives submit to your own husbands as to the Lord.' I need to look at my relationship with Jesus and how I want to submit to Him. That is to be my pattern. As I would do for Jesus, I do for my husband!

## True submission is liberating!

I am released to be free from selfish demands, set on my feet as equal to my husband as a 'daughter of the King'. True submission gives me:

**True submission liberates women**

- True freedom
- Free choice
- The opportunity to be fully me
- Equality
- An attitude of absolute loving surrender 'as to the Lord'.

Wow, what a challenge to my neat little 'loads' of rubbish! My attitude is changed from inside out. I don't need to be scared of that 'S' word anymore!

In practice then, how can I work this out in my life as a wife?

Imagine for a moment that Jesus were to come into your room, here where you are sitting, in physical, touchable form. You know He is present by His spirit, He's promised to be with you and in you, but right now imagine Him physically present. He comes in, smiles at you, kicks off his shoes and sits down. What do you do?

### Attitude 1 - 'I love you'

You express love, appreciation, adoration, worship; you may literally want to 'wash His feet'. All that's in you wells up in thanks and loving delight. He is your Saviour. So, to my husband, being submissive means I am loving and appreciative because it's a response of my heart, a chosen attitude, not simply a duty or a demand. 'Wash my husband's feet?' 'No thanks!' Perhaps not! But think about the attitude of expressive love.

### Attitude 2 - 'What can I do for you, Lord Jesus?'

You immediately want to serve Jesus. To make Him a cup of coffee or His favorite meal, serve Him and care for His needs. Here is your Lord, your Saviour in your house! Get the picture? In the same way, submission means my greatest pleasure is to serve my husband. This attitude touches everything in my life. The work I do, the friends I have, the money I spend, and the clothes I wear. In other words I'm living

*I am not choosing to become a 'non-person' but a person of complete equality,*

to please him. Not out of slavery or subjugation, but because I choose to, freely out of love 'as to the Lord'. In this I am not choosing to become a 'non-person' but a person of complete equality, a helper, one called alongside to compliment and complete.

### Attitude 3 - 'You are the most important person in my life, Lord. I honour you.'

Would I consider shouting at Jesus 'So, you're late again, you're always late!' or; 'I hate you, let me go to my mother?' No way!

The words I say and the tone I say them in is honest and graceful, yet can be totally myself. With Jesus, I never need to 'grin and bear' life and say, 'I'm OK' when I'm not. But His presence and love purifies my tongue. In His company I can relax and unwind, be totally free, laugh, cry, and release my stress and tension. This means that submission 'as to the Lord' involves having exactly the same attitude in the way that I talk to my husband. If I am to honour him, respect, or 'fear' him, my tongue needs to be controlled, 'seasoned with salt' and I need to lovingly and freely be myself.

## 'But you don't know my husband!'

Is this easy? Sometimes yes, sometimes no! It means putting someone else's needs before mine. It's often a direct challenge to my self-attitudes, especially when even the most loving husband is still a sinner, not a saint!

No wife finds it hard to submit to a husband when he takes his headship seriously - laying down his life for her. But there may be days when your husband is far from that ideal. There are days when he is downright awful, frustrating or annoying. When he's forgotten to shave, doesn't notice your needs, demands a meal when you are sick of cooking and then to top it all, wants you to make love at the end of an exhausting day when all you're longing for is sleep! What then?

Sometimes it helps to remember that, as we choose to willingly express love, serve out of love and honour our husband, we are in a very real sense doing this for Jesus. As if the Lord is standing in front of my husband and I am submitting to Him. Remember Jesus said, 'In as much as you did it to the least of my brothers, you did it to me.' That's our liberating privilege; try it and see!

## Taste the spice

- Wives, write down three practical ways you can show your husband Biblical submission:

1. Love
2. Serve
3. Honour

Now decide to put this into practice in attitudes and actions for the next two months. See the difference this makes!

- Husbands, look out for every way to praise her!

### Spice from the Word
*Matthew 25 vs.39-40 - a spice for a wife!*

We know that your husband is not perfect, he is not Jesus. He may be great but there are many times when he behaves far from the model of a head! But notice as I submit I choose to love, serve and honour my husband, it is in fact supreme submission to the King of Kings. 'Whatever you did for the least of these my brothers, you did it for me.'

# 'Any good thing bears repetition'

**The trademark of our marriage ministry over these last eight years has been a large battered green umbrella!** As we were preparing for a seminar on headship and submission it suddenly occurred to Ruthie as an easy-to-remember visual aid of what it means to live as a couple under Biblical headship.

Just as we stand under the umbrella to protect us from the rain, so we stand in Biblical headship and submission to protect us from attack against our marriage. Here is the illustration:

 ### The umbrella is held by the husband.

For whatever reason, God has given the job of headship in the family to the husband. He holds the umbrella. To hold the umbrella firmly he 'sacrifices' one hand. As a biblical husband he chooses to limit his freedom to hold the umbrella.

 ### The wife comes under the umbrella.

It is his wife's choice to step under the protection of the headship held by her husband. Where she steps, the children will step. By choosing to 'submit' to her husband's headship she brings the whole family under the umbrella.

 ### Each tussle over who holds the umbrella.

If there is confusion over the Biblical pattern of headship and submission, the husband and wife can struggle to claim dominance in the marriage. This comes from a misunderstanding of 'head', thinking that it means boss. If the role is properly understood we realize that the one who holds the umbrella is actually less free than the one who doesn't. A wife in true Biblical submission has both hands free to

> *The one who holds the umbrella is actually less free than the one who doesn't.*

express all her gifts and talents, properly promoted by her husband. A husband in true Biblical headship has limited his freedom to hold the umbrella.

## The husband thrusts the umbrella into his wife's hand.

Many husbands abdicate their headship role. They fear to lose their freedom, and so leave their wives to hold the umbrella over the children. They may think they fulfill their obligation as a husband by earning money and bringing it home. They lose out on the privilege of headship and their family loses both a proper husband and father.

Most of us as husbands have to travel away from home. But that does not mean that we have to abdicate our headship. It is as if we keep holding the umbrella but with an elastic arm! We travel but our wives and children know we are still in headship.

Constant contact is kept, by phone, e-mail etc; major decisions are still held until you are together, the husband's thoughts and prayers are constantly 'reaching' home and the wife is constantly 'holding the ladder' for her husband while he is away.

> *Keep holding the umbrella but with an elastic arm!*

## The husband misuses the umbrella to push her down under it.

A domineering husband can misuse his headship, even taking advantage of his wife's submission to push her down out of sight. By doing this he is grossly misusing the responsibility he has. He is making himself vulnerable to attack as he, himself, is not now standing under the God given protection of headship, for he must remember that Christ is his head, for his own protection.

> *By doing this he is grossly misusing the responsibility he has.*

## Both move together under the umbrella to offer protection to others.

In *Ephesians 5 v.32*, Paul talks about the 'profound mystery' of marriage. Amazingly, God has made the institution of marriage a profound illustration of Christ's relationship with His bride, the church.

That is to say that a married couple 'living under the umbrella' of Biblical headship and submission are a profound witness to the world. In fact the wonderful protection of their home and relationship will attract others to come and shelter from the storms of life. What better witness to the world can there be, than a couple prepared to open themselves warmly and securely to the needy neighbors on their road, or the lonely students in the next door apartment, or the desperate families of their church?

> *'living under the umbrella'*

God has so designed marriages to be a demonstration of this care for the world in loving sacrifice, service and compassion. What opportunities we can miss if we fail to live 'under the umbrella'!

 **Spice it this week**

Get hold of the largest umbrella you can find. Open it and stand in front of your long bedroom mirror! Husbands hold the umbrella firmly' over you and your wife.

- Pray together that you will demonstrate Biblical headship and submission in your family life.

- Think who you can invite into your home this week.

- Invite them, have a meal together, don't preach at them, let your lives 'speak'. Be ready to answer any questions they may ask about your life together.

- Think about how you can make your home and marriage relationship an 'umbrella' to needy ones around.

### Spice from the Word
*Colossians 3 vs.15-17 (The Message)*

'Let the peace of Christ keep you in tune with each other, in step with each other. None of this going off and doing your own thing. And cultivate thankfulness. Let the Word of Christ -The Message - have the run of the house. Give it plenty of room in your lives. Instruct and direct one another using good common sense. And sing, sing your hearts out to God! Let every detail of your lives - words, action, whatever be done in the Name of the Master, Jesus, thanking God the Father every step of the way.'

# Had Any Fun Lately?

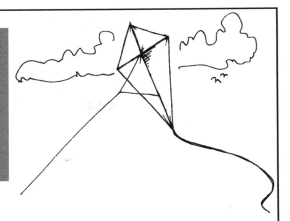

*When Jesus told us to 'become like a little child', he also meant us to have a good look at children and learn!*

Just watch a couple of five-year-olds playing. While we worked at Mahabalipuram we had a house full of families at Cornerstone House and children certainly know how to have fun. They're always on the lookout for it. They play and giggle and chase each other, make sand castles, dig holes and climb trees. They don't need expensive toys. A cardboard box and a few cushions make a great car or aeroplane or space rocket. 'Oh yes' you say, 'That's because they're kids, they've got time.' Have we lost sight of what Jesus said? What's the matter with us? Our lives can get so serious, so busy and so stressful, it seems as if we don't have any time to enjoy ourselves and just have fun. There's something wrong somewhere.

**We don't have any time to enjoy ourselves and just have fun.**

No couple or family should ever get too busy to relax, let go and have fun. This may be the missing ingredient from your marriage. And it is not too late to change it. If we allow time for fun together, we get to know each other more, learn to relate, relax and laugh together and go on building our togetherness and oneness.

## Let's do it now!

Spur of the moment ideas are great fun-value. In our family we love a 'let's do it now' idea. A moonlight picnic for example. It only takes a minute to make a decision to pack a meal into a tiffin, go to a park nearby, or just go up on to the terrace. We have often decided to pack up a basket of food, go to a barren rocky hillside near our house and picnic under the stars. Try a few of these 'do it now' ideas:

- A walk along the beach
- Hire bikes and cycle
- Look at a map and decide to explore a place nearby that you've never been to
- Go for a swim
- Buy ice-creams
- When the monsoon breaks, celebrate by standing outside laughing in the rain, get soaking wet and enjoy it
- Go for a walk as the sun is setting.

It really doesn't matter what we do as long as we all enjoy doing it and have fun away from the struggle to keep up with schedules. Time to laugh, relax and enjoy each other - and the children? They'll just love it too! We are in danger of becoming monotonous and boring if we never do things just for the fun of it.

---

**'Mum and Dad have gone on honeymoon.'**

For some other fun time planning is necessary. Fix a few dates and stick to them, especially if you plan to include a night away from home. Plan at least one 'honeymoon' a year. Just the two of you. Make arrangements for someone to look after the children and have a fun romantic night away for two. You could book into a small hotel for a night or two. Some of our most exciting and delightful times of love have been when we've escaped on 'honeymoon'. Our family are quite used to telling their friends, 'Mum and Dad have gone on honeymoon.'

A change of environment, no phone, no interruptions. We thoroughly recommend it and it's offered to couples very warmly at Cornerstone House, Mahabalipuram! A good way of doing this is to spring it as a surprise on your partner. Make all the arrangements, including someone to look after the children. Ensure the diary is clear. Then whisk him or her away for an exciting weekend! 'We can't afford that sort of thing.' No, but be encouraged that, as your love is mature and growing, you can be wonderfully creative in thinking up fun ideas for one another which cost very little.

---

## As the kite soared, so did her spirit

Aruna and Raj were surrounded by packing boxes. They were due to move to Dubai in two days' time - the truck would be here tomorrow and the house looked bleak, bare stained walls, marks where pictures and posters had hung pressed in on them. They were aching, not just because of the sorting, cleaning, packing and heaving of furniture, but the empty place, and a lot of unknowns weighed very heavily. What had looked like an exciting opportunity three months ago now seemed gloomy. There was still a lot to do, bills to pay, milk to cancel, addresses to change

and friends to ring. The last few days had been hectic. Raj sat down heavily on one of the boxes and looked out of the window. Suddenly he caught sight of a brightly painted kite soaring high above their building. Memories of kite flying, and how he'd loved it as a boy flashed across his mind. 'Come on Aruna, we're going out.'

He grasped her hand and grabbed the door key and ran down the stairs. 'Where are we going?' Aruna asked as she tried to keep up with him weaving in and out of people, parked cars, scooters, children, carts and fruit vendors. 'We're off to fly kites' he called over his shoulder, 'I know just the place.' A few minutes later,

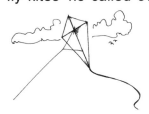

they were on the broad, flat sand of a nearby beach. It was the kite season. Raj bought two, one each. Aruna laughed as she watched her husband racing along the sand to get his kite airborne. 'Hey, this is fun; I haven't done this in years!' As the kite soared, so did her spirit, 'Thanks Lord', she thought out loud, 'You'll get us soaring again soon.'

##  Spice for the week

• Do some 'kite flying'! Write down a list of the things you enjoy doing. Perhaps some you haven't done for years. Fix dates for doing them.

• How about a 'do it now' idea today?

• Plan a 'honeymoon' for this year.

## Spice from the Word
*Song of Songs 6 vs.2-3 & 11*

There is something magnificently healing about being 'ministered to' by God's creatures and creation.

Try to plan time when you can be alone together with the wonders of nature and be still and know that God is God. Few couples ever do this and much that is precious is lost to relationships as a result.

# Release and be free

*Have you done much 'sheet-shaking' recently? Remember Shake the Sheets, when the focus was on the small irritations and hurts that chafe and rub us like sand in the bed?*

**The focus is now not on a day-to-day matter that we need to forgive or be forgiven of but something much deeper or bigger. We may feel, 'I just can't forgive'. We are sure it's gone on too long, dug in too deep, or it's too far in the past.**

## Forgiveness is a choice we make

These types of wounds take many forms. They can be caused by sexual or physical abuse in our childhood, constant failure and rejection in school, homes broken into and treasured memories stolen, a trusted friend breaking our confidence or unfaithfulness in our marriage. Forgiveness is not a feeling. It is a choice we make.

God did that for us. He made a choice in letting His Son be tortured, tormented, kicked, spat on and killed so He could forgive us. We make the decision to forgive or not to forgive. When I say, 'I can't forgive', the truth really is, 'I don't want to', 'I

> **We make the decision to forgive or not to forgive.**

won't' or I haven't yet learned how to'. With the Holy Spirit as our teacher and if we are willing we will be able to do it in the end. It may take time and is not always easy but it's always possible. There is nothing, not one thing in the world that the blood of Christ cannot deal with. If there were, Jesus would have died in vain.

Another excuse we often make is, 'forget it, time heals'. The fact is that time never heals. It may seem that it does sometimes, because details can blur in our memories, but only forgiveness heals truly.

## Learning to Forgive

Tom had a younger brother who was brilliant, clever, a good sportsman, an excellent keyboard player and popular. He was the family favorite. Tom's dad never seemed to recognise that Tom needed praise too. He never quite made the grade. Whatever he did wasn't quite good enough. 'You could do better', 'OK, mostly As, but 2 Bs, improve your marks.'

As Tom grew up and left home, he tried to impress his father with achievements at college, then at work. He was promoted and became an executive director of his company. When he rang to tell his father, hoping for a 'well done, son', all he heard was 'You'll be too busy to come and see us now.' Tom was married to Aruna, happily for the most part. But whenever she made any attempt to express her feelings, he reacted angrily, telling her, 'Stop expecting me to be so perfect.'

What Tom didn't recognise was that the pain in his relationship with his father was affecting his present relationship with Aruna and would continue to do so until he learnt how to forgive, releasing his father and being released himself from the pain attached; cutting the bonds that unforgivingness has on us. In *Luke 6 v.37*, Jesus uses a powerful word in explaining forgiveness, 'pardon (or forgive) and you will be pardoned (or forgiven).'

## Forgiveness is release

The Greek word used for 'release' in the New Testament is 'apolo', release. It is the word that was used when talking about releasing a debtor. Tearing up the bill and saying, 'You don't owe me anything now.' In order to do that we have to be willing to admit that there is a debt that is owed.

*Tearing up the bill and saying, 'You don't owe me anything now.'*

however, wasn't so sure. 'That's just like Dad. He liked me really, he just found it hard to say it, he was busy with work, he couldn't help it.' But in actual fact Tom's father owed him a debt. What debt? - Not reflecting the Father heart of God in constant unconditional love.

Look at Tom again. Aruna sensed that a lot of the source of their problems in their relationship lay in Tom's rejection by his father. Tom,

To work towards that goal is to be the choice of every good father. To love, to support, to be there and to affirm. Tom's father never did that. He owes Tom a debt. Tom needs to first recognise this as a debt and then decide with the love of Jesus and power of the Holy Spirit to tear it up and say, 'You don't owe me anything anymore, I choose to forgive and love you.' In doing this the hurts and rejection have no more power to damage and cannot be transferred into our marriage or any other relationship. This is powerful forgiving!

Jesus taught us to pray, 'Forgive us our debts as we forgive our debtors.' In Tom's case, his father never asked for forgiveness, yet Tom knew that he needed to forgive, not just to be able to love his father, but to be able to truly love Aruna, to live as a released husband. The rejection and unforgivingness have trapped him into the cycle of never feeling quite good enough.

## Letting forgiveness happen

At other times however we may be asked for our forgiveness, and we choose not to because we want to keep punishing the person who has hurt us. We want them to feel a bit of the misery, loneliness, anger or failure that they have inflicted on us.

A month previously David had finally admitted his affair to Jayne. The atmosphere in the house was so heavy and tense, David could hardly stand it a minute longer.

'Letting forgiveness happen'

He'd been back in the house for nearly three weeks now and Jayne had hardly spoken to him. She didn't want him near her. She wanted to punish him for being so cruel to her.

This evening while they were eating silently together he began, 'Jayne, I'm desperately sorry for the way I've hurt you.'

At first Jayne turned away but as David continued and reached across to hold her hand she looked across at him, her eyes full of tears. Loudly, she poured out her pain and hurt of the weeks he'd been away, her anger at the betrayal of her trust, her own sense of failure as a wife.

David listened and held her hand. When she'd finished he moved across to where she was sitting, wrapped his arms around her and she sobbed and sobbed into his shoulder. 'I'm so sorry, I'm so sorry', he kept saying quietly and at last her tears stopped. 'I'd no idea how much I'd hurt you. Will you ever be able to forgive me? Can we really be together again, just like before?'

Jayne sat quiet, stilled now, making the first step as a choice. She held him tightly, 'I do forgive you David' she said, 'It'll be hard to trust you now, I'll need time, but yes I love you and I want us to be together, even more than before.' They hugged again, a long, long, warm hug which spoke more than words.

### Spice it up

Pray and ask the Holy Spirit to show you areas of unforgivingness in your life. This may be painful but trust God's love and sovereign power to hold you as you go through it

Ask God's Holy Spirit to help you forgive and he will bring you to a new release and freedom, a freedom that will add a wonderful spice to your marriage.

### Spice from the Word
_Ephesians 4 vs.26-27_

We are warned clearly in these verses of the way in which the devil can get a foothold in our lives if we allow destructive conflict to remain in our home even for one day! Consider God's 'anger alerts' in _Ps.4 v.4; Ps.37 v.8; Col. 3 v.8 and Eph. 4 v.31._

# Adopted!

**The temperature that day in Pune was over forty. I sat at home with fluttering butterflies, waiting for the familiar drone of Rod's moped to arrive home from the courthouse with news.** Dan aged two and Prilla four were playing on the floor beside me trustingly oblivious to the tension I was feeling.

Suddenly I heard the clang of our gate and a whoop of delight. 'We've done it', Rod bounded up the steps and ran through the front door with a beaming smile, little rivers of sweat trickling off his beard, waving 'five star' bars for everyone. 'Wow,' he said, 'this is the first time I've been in labour!' I knew what he meant. We now had Prilla legally ours, adopted into our family, four years old and definitely one of us.

Eight years later, rain lashed against the windows on a monsoon afternoon. It was the first day of term at Hebron School in Ooty where we worked. Our house was full of chatter and laughter, students, parents and friends coming and going. Our pastor, helmet in hand, walked in looking concerned, 'Ruthie, a baby has been abandoned in the church.'

*Two kilos of precious humanity*

In that instant, against all seeming logic of the moment I knew this was what I had been praying for. Prilla's ears instantly pricked up, 'Can I go and bring him home Mum, please? I can go on the pastor's scooter, please let me go.' Making cups of coffee in our kitchen I was keeping an ear open for Prilla's voice. Banging, the front door swung open and a very damp yet glowing Prilla danced through the door. 'Mum! I've got him, look!' Her eyes spoke volumes as she handed him over to me. A tiny bundle wrapped in an old purple sweater. He was here.

The room was packed, everyone pushing forward to have a glimpse of this tiny unexpected arrival. A newborn baby, cord still intact, one screwed up little face, perfect, ten fingers, ten toes and a thatch of thick black hair, two kilos of precious humanity. Once again a baby was 'born' into our family by adoption.

## Love is something we do

I remember looking at Ben our second son just after he was born. To us he was absolutely beautiful. Yet his face looked as if it had come off badly in a boxing match. He seemed to have no neck and his eyes look squinted. However he was ours and because he was ours we adored him. That love is unconditional; it is not related to looks or behavior.

Yet in the same way the love which we have for Prilla and for Ande is teaching Rod and me about the fatherly love of God, his adoption love for us. It is equally committing and regardless of the cost.

## Is it all easy?

Sounds great, but you may be thinking, is it so easy? No, if it all sounds like smooth sailing we are not being honest. At times I have felt like a coiled spring inside, ready to pounce because my patience has been stretched to breaking point.

In the early months when we first had Prilla there was so much unknown about her. The four years before she became part of our family were a mist of history which we could not humanly experience with her, topped by the sense of guilt that I was finding it tough.

Yet to balance all that was the fun and fascination of seeing her develop, with her unique, sparkling temperament. Unconditional love comes as a choice. It may begin as an act of will and suddenly

### Love-choosing

*There are two ways that a baby may be born to you, the first, the gift of a child through your love-making, the second, the gift of a child through your love-choosing.*

*Receiving the gift of a child into your lives by adoption means the child is equally and totally yours - just in the same way as a natural born baby is. In fact in some amazing way, he or she belongs even more as you have chosen this child. Adoption comes from the father heart of God. If we are his sons and daughters we are adopted into his family Do we really know what this means?*

*It's powerful. When Paul wrote, 'we have received the spirit of adoption so we cry Abba father (daddy, my daddy)'; he was speaking out of the Greco-Roman culture of his day. His culture understood that a son was deliberately chosen by his adopted father to perpetuate his name and inherit his estate. In no way, not even to the smallest degree, was this adopted son inferior to a son born naturally.*

*F. F. Bruce says, 'In fact the adopted son might well enjoy his father's affection more fully and reproduce the father's character more worthily.' Paul was also Jewish and with my own Jewish roots I delight in the fact that Jewish adoption is irrevocable. No matter what, however terrible, however dishonoring or disappointing an adopted son or daughter becomes, they cannot be disinherited. Certainly, you can tell a natural child to leave home or 'don't let me see your face again', but an adopted child, never!*

*The essence of our adoption is security, love, belonging and trust. We are not slaves or second-best children, but heirs, full heirs of all the rich inheritance of our faith. What an incredible relationship to have.*

it is there as an emotion.

Any parenting has pleasure and pain. Dirty diapers, running noses, disobedience, poor marks in school and accidents; we are not going to be protected from these because we have given birth in a natural way. Just because we don't know the history or past inheritance of an adopted child, is that a reason to fear? We know all too well the temperament faults that our natural born children may inherit from us, our parents or grandparents!

## The Adoption Process

The procedure for legal guardianship and adoption is fairly complex. It may take many hours in the court and with social workers. There will be home visits, surprise drop-ins and reports to write. In our case both Prilla and Ande were living in our family while the legal procedures took place. Both cases, although totally different, took about nine months before the final papers were through; a fairly normal length of 'pregnancy'! The local Social Welfare Department will give all the details of up-to-date adoption procedures.

### Spice it this week

It is often fear of the unknown or what people or family may say that stops us from acting in faith and reflecting God's father-heart.

Four Steps Forward towards Adoption

- Pray together and wait until you are both agreed.
- Investigate the local Social Welfare Department to find out how to proceed with adoption in your area.
- Visit local hospitals, clinics or Children's Homes where children may be available for adoption. Leave your name and address for contact at any time.
- Talk about adoption wisely to friends and family, remembering that prejudices and the fear of the unknown should not be a deciding factor.

At the time when Rod began to feel he could safely say goodbye to the 'terrible twos', forget disturbed nights and pack away train sets for grandchildren, Ande has brought him back to the starting line! Yes it can be tiring and demanding, but it is also exhilarating and challenging. Recently Rod and Ande had just walked in from an evening stroll to the garage and teashop across the road. I asked Ande, 'What were you and dad doing?' He looked up at me as if I really ought to have known, 'Dad and I were talking, just talking!' Abba, father, Daddy, my Daddy.

### Spice from the Word _Galatians 4 vs.3-7_

In these verses God shows us that we are all adopted by Him, our perfect Father. The whole Bible is about God's perfect love for us, His sacrifice, His longing to bring us back into relationship with Him. Remember the story of the Prodigal Son; how the father picks up his robes and runs towards his son, this is how much our adoptive Father loves us.

If this chapter has spoken to you, if you are already an adoptive parent, have faith in God who gives us the blueprint for adoption. Be encouraged to consider the joys and challenge of being an adoptive parent and ask for his wisdom in the decisions you make.

# Body Talk

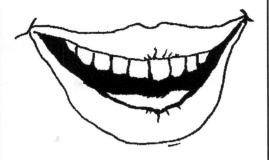

*'Your body shouts before your lips can speak' says author Leil Lawndes, a writer on relationships. Similarly a drama teacher watching some bad acting shouts in exasperation 'No, no that's not what you're saying.'*

*Every tiny movement, every body position divulges your private thoughts. The way you move is your 'autobiography in motion'. We can draw people, particularly our husband or wife, to us or push them away, by all the small actions and reactions zipping between us.*

## That 'gut feeling'

God created us to communicate, to be in touch with one another, and He gives us bodies to show it. Most of us at some time have sensed or had a 'gut feeling' **'Our body speaks louder than words'** that someone is telling us a lie. What we really mean is that their body language and their spoken words do not agree.

If our husband is listening to us with his head down and his arms crossed against his chest we would soon sense he was not with us, or agreeing with something we said. Often women seem to have a stronger ability to pick up and decipher small non-verbal signals. That is why few husbands can pull the wool over their wife's eyes, without her realizing it!

As 'our body speaks louder than words' a look at some of these gestures may help us to understand why we have difficulty with our communication:

- Reinforced arm cross - closed fist - showing a hostile attitude.
- Arm gripping. A firm stand taken here.
- Defensive standing position.
- Maybe someday you will be as intelligent as me.

## Honouring with our bodies

*Psalm 139* beautifully describes the wonder of our bodies being created, perfectly and uniquely, in secret. In *2 Corinthians 6 v.16* the picture is of our body being the temple, the dwelling place of the Holy Spirit.

We also promise in our marriage vows, 'with my body I honour you'- this is not only in my physical love-making but how I communicate honour, love and respect with my body to you.

It is outside the realm of this book to do a full study on body language, however if we grasp the importance of our eyes, mouth and hands we will change gear into richer communication.

### Hands - 'I'm receiving you'

Tightened fists and locked arms give clear 'fight or defend' signals. Sometimes in a discussion or argument together we unconsciously tighten a fist. Try to practise relaxing your hands, palms up and open with body, and say 'I'm listening and receiving you loud and clear.'

**Palms up**

### Eyes - 'I have eyes only for you'

'Look at me when I'm speaking to you', every child has heard that phrase! I remember telling one of our sons when he was around 5 years old, 'Look and see what color your Uncle Dan's eyes are when you say 'hello' to him'. Why? So he would make eye contact. When we keep making eye contact with our wife or husband it says,

'I have eyes only for you.'
'I can't take my eyes off you.'
'I'm listening to you alone.'

**Make eye contact**

Make eye contact not only when you are together but across a crowded room, in a bus, in church or at an office party. Medical research has recently discovered that intense eye contact releases a specific chemical into our bloodstream. This hormone is detected when we feel 'in love'; so keep it flowing!

### Mouth - 'Smile, I love you'

'Your smile lights up the room'. A smile eases tension, relaxes the giver and the receiver and can radiate joy. Watch children; small children smile or laugh on average every four minutes. An adult smiles or laughs on average twelve times a day! What happened to us?

**A smile eases tension**

### Spice for this week

Smile at each other first thing in the morning, at breakfast, as you leave for work, as soon as you come into the house, last thing at night, with the family, as often as you can. Watch the response in your beloved's eyes! Also practice the other body signals, eye contact and your hand positions.

## Read Psalm 139 together:

Lord, you have examined me and know all about me.
You know when I sit down and when I get up.
You know my thoughts before I think them.
You know where I go and where I lie down.
You know thoroughly everything I do.
Lord, even before I say a word, you already know it.
You are all around me - in front and at the back - and have put your hand on me.
Your knowledge is amazing to me; it is more than I can understand.
Where can I go to get away from your Holy Spirit?
Where can I run from you?
If I go up to the heavens, you are there.
If lie down in the grave, you are there.
If I rise with the sun in the east and settle in the west beyond the sea, even there you would guide me.
With your right hand you would hold me.

I could say, 'The darkness will hide me.
Let the light around me turn into night.'
But even the darkness is not dark to you.
The night is as light as the day; darkness and light are the same to you.
You made my whole being; you formed me in my mother's body.
I praise you because you made me in an amazing and wonderful way.
What you have done is wonderful.
I know this very well.
You saw my bones being formed as I took shape inside my mother's body.
When I was put together there, you saw my body as it was formed.
All the days planned for me were written in your book before I was one day old.
God, your thoughts are precious to me. There are so many!
If I could count them they would be more than all the grains of sand.
When I wake up, I am still with you.

---

 ## Spice from the Word
_Song of Songs 1 v.12 to 2 v.7_

Consider chapter 1 v15 -'Your eyes are doves.' Eyes speak! They are very important in easy communication. It's hard to talk to someone who is avoiding eye contact even though it may be more culturally accepted in some places.

Compare this verse with _Matthew 3 v.16_, and _10 v.16_. Our eyes should reflect gentleness, purity and holiness. Doves can only see straight in front of themselves, not to their sides, in the same way we need to be completely focused. The other interesting thing about doves is that they are extremely faithful, only mating with the same doves their whole lives. If the other dove dies they will never mate again. We in the same way need to be completely faithful.

# Creative Conflict

## Exasperation

In the first few years of our marriage I would try and avoid conflict at all costs, yet I couldn't. Some conflict exasperated me. Ruthie said what she felt. I didn't. She wanted to talk it all out. I couldn't. She had very high expectations. I hadn't thought about them. She wanted to say sorry. I decided I couldn't. For me conflict was a constant process of either trying to win, or trying to smooth over, at the very least trying to avoid a repeat! It was a most unsatisfactory attitude, as  every disagreement became what I called 'a heavy', and often resulted in me simmering with anger and Ruthie exploding into tears! Of course we had plenty of happy times in between, but the 'heavies' could droop heavily over several days if we were not careful.

## Avoid Conflict? - No!

Does any of that sound a bit familiar? **It took me several years to learn that conflict in our marriage was not necessarily something I had to fight and avoid**. It was something God could use to bring Ruthie and me closer to each other, as well as being a way he could use to teach me, particularly, how to say sorry.

As my attitude gradually began to change, so I found that conflict became less and less of a heavy black cloud and increasingly I saw it as an opportunity to learn how to be a more resourceful and valuable person to Ruthie. I also began to learn how to say sorry, a word I never managed to get past my lips before I was married.

# Dynamic Growth, NOT Static Isolation

It's not that I now lick my lips at the prospect of a good fight! But it has no longer become a battle I have to win or a bomb I have to avoid. How has this happened? In reflection, I think I can identify several important growth points:

1. Firstly, I realized our marriage was in dynamic growth and not static isolation. Yesterday's ways of relating together need not be the ways of tomorrow. I can change, my will can change. This is the wonderful work of the Holy Spirit. We are not necessarily trapped into a personality type, culture or social habit. Growth is going on and conflict is inevitable as we grow and change - not necessarily in proportion to our growth, but it will occur as an outcome of growth.

2. Secondly, I appreciated our differences. Ruthie and I are at  opposite ends of the scale in the way we respond to conflict. Ruthie is more like a pressure cooker and as the heat increases so does the pressure until an explosion of steam occurs! I on the other hand, am more like a covered pot with cracks. I simmer away, letting off steam with maybe sarcastic remarks or sullen behavior. But we need not be type-cast like that. Ruthie has learnt to control the 'explosions'  and I have learnt to let off steam in a more constructive way. We ARE changing; in fact Ruthie likes to boast that she is married to a new person everyday!

3. Thirdly, I have learnt the joy and value of resolution. Somehow I had grown up thinking that the weak said sorry and the loser apologized. From God's point of view, nothing could be further from the truth. It is actually a much tougher, stronger thing to say sorry, you become a bigger man than your ego! I've still got big lessons to learn in this area, but at least I've started.

---

Read *Matthew 7 v5.3-5* (his speech etc.), *Matthew 6 v5.14 & 15* (forgive sins) and *Matthew 5 v.9.*

Here are a few practical suggestions on how to allow your conflict to be creative rather than destructive.

• Don't try and resolve conflicts while either one of you is hungry or tired. Emotions are much more fragile when the blood sugar is low.

- Decide beforehand not to raise your voice or tone, but try to keep calm and controlled. You'll be surprised how a little control here will prevent excesses even physically.

'Stay calm'

- Do not walk away or out in the middle of a conflict. Let tears come if they need to, determine to see it through.

'Definitely tomorrow Lord...'

- Do try to resolve the conflict before you sleep; this is a good Biblical principle. However, if you are too tired, agree together to lay it down and agree together to deal with it the next day.

- Decide to be the first one to say sorry and mean it! That's a hard one for me, as you can guess. In our conflicts 99 times out of 100 Ruthie gets there well before me, but I'm trying.

- After you have said sorry and the conflict has subsided, decide to have a 'listening to understand' on the issue that sparked the conflict, as soon as is practical.

## Spice it this week

Analyze the way you usually deal with conflict between yourselves. Write down three or four practical ways in which you could resolve it more quickly.

## Spice from the Word
*Song of Songs 6 vs.1-12 and 1 Peter 3 vs.7-9*

As the lovers in Song of Songs find themselves in conflict with each other we see a resolution that works. In the time between their problem and resolution two fundamental attitudes are revealed. She concentrates on his strengths. He responds to insult with blessing. A similar principle is found in *1 Peter 3 vs.7-9*.

# Love Letters

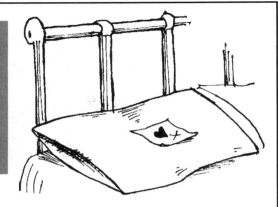

*'We are well past that kind of romantic stuff'*

*'In our culture we don't write love letters'*

*'Love letters? - Just teenage infatuation'*

Do you find yourself thinking things like this when you are faced with a spice like 'Love Letters'? If you do, join the club. I'm afraid I have done the same thing and that is why Ruthie insists that I write this week.

We'd been married a few months and I had to go away for a few days. That night as I removed my pyjamas from the bag my new bride had so lovingly packed for me, out fell a small piece of paper. I picked it up curiously to find a 'love letter'! Just a few words signed with a big R and X. My heart did a little skip. I slept with a smile that night!

## Love grows by being cultivated

Love letters are not a modern invention. They are found in the most ancient of literature. In fact, the centre book of the Bible is a love letter, the Song of Solomon. True, the Song of Solomon can be interpreted as a type of God's love for the church but it is basically a very explicit and unabashed love letter between King Solomon and his Shulamite bride.

If God can endorse love letters in His word, who am I to push them aside? The fact is that love grows by being cultivated. It does not always spring automatically from the sparkle in her eyes! Love is a discipline and is worked at. Neglect love and it will die like a plant without water. Cultivate it, nourish it, stimulate it and it will blossom, multiply and bless you. The Bible does not condemn us for love; it commands us to love.

## God's love letter to us

One of the best ways of strengthening our love for the Lord is by reading and meditating on His love letters to us - the Bible. The whole of the Bible is in some sense, God's expression of His love for us. It is a pouring out of His heart. My love for the Lord grows as I discover new things in His word each day; and so in a similar way, my love for my wife or husband will grow - by communicating love. Communicating in words - written words - can go a long way. Some of us have difficulty in being able to explain ourselves in spoken words. Many men are like that. We can be those 'strong silent' types, the 'dark horse' or the 'mystery man'. Our wives have a lot of difficulty in discovering what we think or feel about things. We may find it difficult even to express these little words our wives are longing for - 'I love you', so try writing. You don't have to be a Shakespeare to put a few words on a card! One lunch hour at a greetings card shop could set you up for several months of love letters, especially if you eventually add or change a few words. Go for it, you silent man!

*Go for it, you silent man!*

---

 ## Spice it this week

Try some of the following:
- Write a poem using the image of a garden for a wife or the image of a strong tower for a husband.
- Have fun hiding little love notes to each other in unusual places.
- Write fun limericks to each other. This is an excellent .way to endure a boring meeting. Just make sure you don't burst out laughing while doing it! For example:

'Try singing it'

> There was a bald husband of mine
> Whose pate had a glorious shine
> When he bends his head low
> Did I catch a halo?
> For to me, he is all but divine!

- Surprise her with a coded letter in the personal column of newspaper
- Send him a love text message
- Leave a little note on his or her pillow, in their bag, or even in the fridge!

---

 ## Spice from the Word
*Song of Songs 4 vs.1-7*

The Bridegroom praises seven aspects of his beloved's beauty, the number of perfection. It is genuine appreciation of her physical beauty. Remember God as Creator has made each aspect of His creation a masterpiece of art. We can marvel at being male and female. Let these images inspire you to write or speak words to each other describing the beauty of one another's physical being.

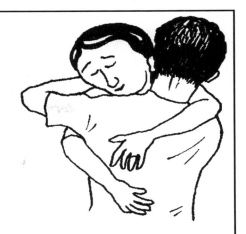

# In Sickness and in Health, For Better For Worse

*The phone rang; it was Sam. 'Are you busy? We need you to pray. It's Rachel, she is so low again, feeling rotten. I don't know how to help.' For months Rachel had been unwell. The hospital had run all the tests possible and nothing seemed to show up. Rachel felt constantly exhausted, listless and afraid that she just couldn't drag herself through another day.*

*Sam felt very discouraged. He needed Rachel to be the healthy, strong and capable girl that he married. He relied on her wisdom, energy and spiritual insight. This fearful, tearful wife was like a stranger to him. He wanted to fix her, to make her better, to do something, anything practical that altered the situation. However, there are times when the right thing to do is nothing except 'be there'. When Rachel cried out her frustration, that her body would not cooperate with her spirit and will, she sobbed 'Sam, you can't do anything, just be there, hold me, give me time.'*

***The best way to be there is often by giving a loving hug. To lovingly hold one another patiently waiting, without words.***

When our first baby boy was stillborn, we'd been married one year. We were fulfilled, energetic, thrilled with the challenges of our ministry in schools and camps, excited by the prospect of being parents. Then it happened. Totally unexpected. Instead of the cradle beside my bed in the hospital holding our little baby boy, our arms were empty. As the doctor wheeled me back to the room with Rod holding my hand, he wisely looked at Rod and said 'I have done all I can. Please push these two beds close together and hold one another.'

**Just 'be there'**

A simple yet profound prescription for broken bodies and broken hearts - 'just be there'.

The worst pain comes from loneliness, feeling isolated from others by sickness, depression, or just being run down. As I sobbed, feeling an ache of despair and disappointment, deeper than anything I'd ever felt before, Rod just held me and as he wept, I held him.

## 'I am with you always'

God knows that so well. This is why Jesus' rich words of assurance, 'Surely I am with you always', are so powerful. The promise of our comforter, the Holy Spirit, is to be present with us forever. Emmanuel 'God with us', our creator has made us like this and He is 'just there' always. Gillian Warren says 'Comfort, true comfort, comes alongside someone being the way they are feeling, what they are feeling, sharing their hurt or grief or disappointment - and that's all.'

## No quick, easy solution

Naturally when there is pain or disappointment, we want a solution but there is no quick solution. Someone dies, you lose a job, you don't get a promotion, a friend gets cancer, and there is no easy answer. It's tempting to react by trying to give a quick 'cheer up' fix.

'Come on, it's not that bad'
'Lots of people have far worse problems'

We are guilty sometimes of ignoring our partner's distress, and quoting a verse of Scripture, which may just not be appropriate right then.

I remember a well-meaning friend coming to visit me after our baby died. Pushing a book into my hands, 'Ruthie, you must read this, it is excellent, all about gaining through losing.' Ouch! – It hurt. I didn't want to read about anything right then, I wasn't even asking any questions. All I could do was lean on Rod and the tangible presence of  Emmanuel. I needed time.

Yet to 'be there' for each other does also mean more than silent comfort, reassurance and long hugs. It also means a willingness to go on together, walking through mists of pain or uncertainty. To face the future with courage, knowing God in new ways as our Emmanuel His awesome Presence.

## Receiving through others

As we walk together and hold one another through our pain we can then meaningfully begin to analyze the situation or ask why? We may need to draw others in to hold us up in prayer, to support us; to hear God's voice in His word for us; to ring us up, to bring a meal to our house; to care in lots of practical ways. Sometimes we have to humble ourselves and ask that we can be held when we want to look as if we can cope. Remember to protect your loved one from an overkill of too many well-meaning visitors, especially those who give advice or yet another remedy.

## Serve one another

Just being there gives us opportunity to serve another in very intimate ways, to give those extra touches, to care and say 'I love you'.

> *Sanjiv came home early. He burst into the flat, slammed the door and threw his briefcase on to the table. Rema knew something was wrong.*
>
> *'Has it been a bad day?' she asked.*
>
> *'Too right it has. Rajiv has got the promotion. I can't believe it. Think of all the extra hours I put in.'*
>
> *Sanjiv was angry, very angry, but underneath he was hurt.*
>
> *'I'm so sorry, my love' said Rema, putting her arms round him as he sat slumped in a chair at the table.*
>
> *'You must be so disappointed', she said. She sat down beside him and gradually his anger subsided. It was what he needed, for her to be there, and slowly he began to feel comforted. He was now ready to talk and pray.*

For example, when your husband or wife or one of the children is sick, especially if it is for a longer length of time, make a special effort to break the monotony of the day. Arrange a tray with a few fresh flowers, a little note or joke tucked under the plate. A small portion of tasty food well presented makes such a difference to a sick person's appetite. Keep the bedroom tidy, clean sheets and pillowcases every day, and a good supply of books, magazines and music, if they like that.

## Spice It Up Together

Next time there is sickness, disappointment, pain, just 'be there'. Your comforting presence is needed first; words come later. Practice the 'long hug', Hold each other for at least 20 seconds. This says 'I'm here and I love you and will never abandon you'. We needn't wait just for the very painful moments. Make it a regular 'spice'.

## Spice from the Word
### 2 Corinthians 12 vs. 9-10

Paul could say what he did in v.10 because of what God had told him to do in v.9! That's fine for Paul, but what about us! When we are weak or sick it's tempting to feel self-pity. Allowed to fester, self-pity spreads like a poison (Hebrews 12 v.15) it neutralizes the power of God's Spirit in our lives and cuts us off from the grace God promises to provide. Don't let self-pity rule. Love one another with the strong compassion of God in the tough times.

# Historically Yours

**A friend of mine once told us, 'The trouble with my wife is that when she gets angry, she gets so historical!'** We thought he'd got the word wrong, 'You mean she gets hysterical?' 'No, no' he clarified, 'she gets historical; she keeps bringing up the past and using it against me.'

## Condemned by history

Key historical phrases that can really damage a marriage are: 'you always...' or 'I knew it!' Such phrases assume there will be no change. What there was in the beginning, there is now, and ever shall be, a world without end! Such phrases condemn us to being stuck at our worst, all the time, and where there is no expectation of change, it usually does not occur.

*And where there is no expectation of change, it usually does not occur.*

Words or phrases that are 'history' are guaranteed to raise your beloved's blood pressure! You will be in for combat rather than conversation. Remember these:

- 'Always' (You always forget to take Asha to tuition)
- 'Never' (You're never ready)
- 'Why don't you ever...?' (Why don't you ever stop talking?)
- 'You're just like your mother!' (or father)

Yet our God is totally the opposite. He is supremely optimistic, and supremely creative. He is constantly at work building his kingdom, creating and changing us from glory to glory, believe it or not. Ruthie is fond of saying that she is married to a new man every twenty-four hours! I'd love to think that a new man is always an improvement on the old man, but I'm afraid that isn't always the case. But whatever, her constant expectations of me keep challenging me to move forward or at least to stay put!

## Letting go of history

A couple had a particular problem with 'history'. She would use his past to rub salt into the wounds of the present:

'You get angry because you have never been able to control your temper. I've never known you any different. Even our first night you got angry.'

He would use her past to excuse his own failings in the present: 'You had a friendship with that fellow since before we got married. I married you knowing all that. Why should you get so upset over my feelings with this girl now?'

> **He would use her past to excuse his own failings in the present**

The major problem with keeping 'history' alive is that we never really learn to forgive each other. We hold on to hidden weapons and can too easily be tempted to pull them out of our arsenal when the battle 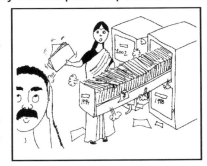 gets tough. We can keep hurting each other with the same weapon again and again, each time pushing it in deeper and deeper. We can think, 'If I don't remind him of what he's done, he'll never learn, and he'll never change.' The truth is that the more we remind each other, the more we cannot change.

Have you ever noticed how in the Old Testament the Lord lays great emphasis on the marvellous and wonderful things he has done for his people, rather than using their past failings as a stick to beat them with?

The only real answer to past failures is not simply to try to forget about them. We need to draw them out, like arrows from a wound, and then break them, through healing forgiveness from one another, and to one another.

## Good memories

A great few verses to look at together this week are:
*Deuteronomy 8 vs.2-10.*
'Remember how the Lord your God has led you in the desert for these forty years, taking away your pride and testing you, because he wanted to know

what was in your heart. He wanted to know if you would obey his commands. He took away your pride when he let you get hungry, and then he fed you with manna, which neither you nor your ancestors had ever seen. This was to teach you that a person does not live by eating only bread, but by everything the Lord says. During these forty years, your clothes did not wear out, and your feet did not swell. Know in your heart that the Lord your God corrects you as a parent corrects a child.'

'Obey the commands of the Lord your God, living as he has commanded you, and respect him. The Lord your God is bringing you into a good land that has wheat and barley, vines, fig trees, pomegranates, olive oil and honey. It is a land where you will have plenty of food, where the rocks are iron, and where you can dig copper out of the hills.'

'When you have all you want to eat, then praise the Lord your God for giving you a good land.'

Read it and ponder over your Father's involvement in every part of your own history as a family. Remind each other of the wonderful life-changing things God has done for both of you, especially this past year.

## Spice it up!

Go back over last week and count the number of instances when you used a 'historical phrase' with one another. Count the times you thought them without saying them! Write them down on a separate piece of paper. Decide not to use them in the future. As a visual aid of this decision go to the kitchen and burn the piece of paper - let the past be past/finished/gone!

Remind each other of the good, great and wonderful things God has done for both you and your family.

## Spice from the Word
*James 5 v.16*

Unconfessed guilt from the past is a guarantee of an unstable life. The cracks and flaws and tripwires keep us tense and wondering when history will catch up with us. This can be dealt with as we 'clean house' and choose to be honest, to forgive and be forgiven. Confessing our faults opens up our lives to God's healing power.

# Signals of Faithfulness

Peter the youth pastor walked in and sat down on a couch. The room was crowded with young people. The music was loud, the atmosphere relaxed, loud laughter and animated discussions on cricket, fashion, plans for the youth club picnic next week filled the air.

Peter's wife Anna was busy making cups of coffee and talking to Sam and Vinod who were putting out cups, sugar and biscuits. Anna had completed an important arrangement in the office today, but now she was tired. Peter was tired too, he'd had a difficult day, so many demands on his time and a misunderstanding with the elders over what dress code was acceptable for the youth in the church had frustrated him.

Sally and Priya came and sat down beside him, 'How are you. Uncle?' they chirped. They always called him Uncle even though they were only a couple of years younger than he was and the same age as Anna.

*He hadn't noticed her, looked at her, spoken to her or touched her the whole evening.*

Peter leaned back and shut his eyes, smiled and listened as they chatted on about college classes. One or two others joined them and Peter leaned down, picked up his guitar and absentmindedly began to strum. Half-an-hour later Anna walked past, stepping over legs and coffee cups. She glanced down at Peter who was now in deep conversation with Sally and Priya. Others were relaxing, and a game of Settlers was in full swing.

Three hours later as the last person left the house, Anna felt drained. Not that she was so physically tired but just empty somehow as if her presence was unimportant to Peter. He hadn't noticed her, looked at her, spoken to her or touched her the whole evening. She felt disconnected and knew this was a usual feeling after an 'open house'. Somehow she felt uneasy about Priya, what was the matter with her, she trusted Peter but somehow...?

## What Signals were missing?

What is that special ingredient that makes a couple look so 'together'? What is it that gives a strong sense of faithfulness and love between them? What warns intruders that even though they are going to be welcomed into a home with love and friendship this marriage is secure? What signals were missing between Peter and Anna?

A month later Anna confronted Peter. This particular evening he had spent the whole evening sitting on the floor teaching Priya and Aruna the guitar. Priya had rung six times this week often asking to speak to Peter, and when Anna had tried to chat to her she seemed disinterested. During the open house Anna had once again felt ignored,  and then angry and finally afraid that Priya, her friend, was becoming an 'intruder' and their relationship was at risk. Peter was shocked at the intensity of Anita's feelings. His reactions were typical 'How can you doubt me?', 'I'd never look at another woman', 'Don't be so suspicious.'

They realized that they needed to choose to invest time and thought into connecting closely together and giving strong signals of faithfulness to others. Whether we've been married two years or twenty years we need to keep reassuring each other of our faithful promise 'that forsaking all others I choose you' and as we do that, to communicate signals of faithfulness to others.

However, the following week he agreed to talk this through with an older couple to whom they'd chosen to be accountable. Following this they decided to put in place some clear signals of faithfulness.

## Keep these signals flashing

1. Make eye contact with one another as often as possible

2. When coming home, whatever .is happening or whoever is at home greet your partner first.

3. Have some secret signal that means 'I love you' i.e. rubbing the bridge of your nose or pulling your left ear lobe. Be inventive - a touch of James Bond is needed here! '

4. Laugh freely together

5. Affirm one another clearly to others. Make a point of saying something good about your husband or wife in public. If they look attractive, tell them and others. Express your love and delight in your partner.

6. Keep yourself accountable of your time and place to one another.

7. See that you are the top person in one another's list of VIPs and that others know it too.

### This Week's Spice

Some of the above list may be particularly important to you.

Decide three signals of faithfulness personal to your relationship. Practise them in the light of *Proverbs 3 v.3*: 'Let love and faithfulness never leave you, bind them around your neck, write them on the tablet of your heart.'

### Spice from the Word
*Song of Songs 8 vs.5-7 and Exodus 39 v.14*

'Place me like a seal over your heart, like a seal in your arm' (*Song of Songs 8 v.6*). This is the cry of a contented lover who longs for oneness, security, delight, fulfillment, wanting this sense of belonging to last forever. The lover desires to be set as a seal on her husband's heart, the centre of his affection; to be as a seal on his arm is to experience his strength and protection publicly, a signal of faithfulness.

A seal is a mark of authenticity that can be used by only one person. This is also the way God wants us to be with him, read *Exodus 39 v.14*.

# Pillars of Affirmation

Affirmation matters, we all know this. We need affirmation, especially words of praise or appreciation and meaningful encouragement said about something specific. In all our relationships, it makes an outstanding difference but nowhere as powerfully as in our marriage.

**Just look at Jacob and Reena - they've been married for only a few weeks, look at how they watch each other. Reena is glowing as Jacob notices and affirms her beauty, her business and organization skills and her cooking. Jacob seems to have grown a couple of feet as Reena admires his athletic body, attractive smile and integrity.** In ten years' time will they have let this lapse? Will they just carry on day-to-day life, exchanging information in a business-like way? How about in twenty years' time?

## Affirmation never gets old

Even when energy fades and hair turns grey affirmation never gets old. True, sincere and creative affirmation sustains us through the years, both in rough patches and in the best moments in our marriage. Affirmation is a tool, which, well used can build our marriage immensely.

## 'What's he really saying?'

However there are also wrong ways to use this tool which we need to watch out for, where we selfishly use sweet talk to get what we want. Nobody likes being manipulated least of all in a marriage.

A husband who tells his wife she is beautiful just when he wants to make love with her is manipulative. A wife who praises her husband's practical skills only when she wants some work done in the house, is manipulative. So in order to use this tool effectively we need to be a craftsman who knows his tool and his material. A carpenter feels the grain of the wood and chisels into the grain bringing out the depth, quality and color. A goldsmith turns and shapes with minute precision the exquisite gold earring he is holding over the heat with delicate and intricate skill. He crafts the gold design to fit the shape of the jewel.

'Like apples of gold in settings of silver is a word spoken in right circumstance', *Proverbs 25 v.11*. Ask yourself if there is an area of your husband's or wife's life that needs strengthening or encouraging, in order to discover daily what needs affirmation and not take one another for granted. Observe one another, pay attention to what matters to each other, what disturbs your partner or fires his or her enthusiasm. Increase your knowledge of each other and remember we are always changing.

## Knowing each other now

*Rod and I have celebrated our thirty fourth wedding anniversary and yet I often say, 'I am married to a new man everyday!' We need to keep on increasing in understanding. Peter the married apostle says 'live with your wife with knowledge' 1 Peter 3 v.7. He probably did a lot of affirming! Are we paying attention to one another? Many wives stop really observing and learning about their husbands once the children are born. We focus all our attention, time and energy into meeting their needs. Husbands get so preoccupied with work that their wives become simply a delicious body in bed or gourmet cook in the kitchen!*

## Shaping the Jewel

It may help to be able to isolate the four areas in our lives that need affirmation from one another, mental, social, physical and spiritual. Rather like four facets of a piece of jewelry, each needs to be polished and well shaped to become an exquisite display of beauty.

Consider Reena again as a beautiful young wife. She knows she is attractive and enjoys having Jacob complimenting her wonderful eyes and beautiful smile. However, recently she has felt inept socially as if people enjoy her company only because she is good looking; therefore Jacob needed to affirm and encourage her in the <u>social area</u> of her life. 'I like the way you reached out to that stranger', 'You are a wonderful listener.' It meets her need right now.

Jacob has always been confident of his academic ability. As a boy he constantly achieved first rank. When Reena affirms him in this area,

'You really are great',

'You think through issues so fast',

'It's amazing how you remember the details of everything you read', he appreciates it but longs for her affirmation of his spiritual growth.

'I can see God is changing you',

'You are so quick to forgive me - I really appreciate that',

'I am so grateful that you remind us to pray together'. By affirming Jacob in this area of his life Reena is using the tool of affirmation effectively on the jewel that is her husband.

In order to recognise each other's needs we need to recognise our own needs and be willing to talk honestly about the areas in which we feel fearful and inadequate. We are there for one another. We can't expect each other always to be mind readers and so we need to be honest and real.

## Spice it up this week

Take time alone to think about your partner's life right now. Which area in his or her life most needs your attention and affirmation? Write down the four areas:

Mental,

Physical,

Spiritual,

Social

Think how you would affirm specifically. Write down the actual words that you could say. Think of as many ways as you can to affirm in the right area and write them down. Make sure you do it this week. You could turn affirmations into a love letter - just see that jewel sparkle!

## Spice from the Word
*Ephesians 6 vs.12-18*

The Bible urges us to be alert to spiritual forces of darkness pitted against the pillars of our marriage. It is essential that we put on armor and keep alert in daily spiritual warfare (Eph. 6 v.18), encourage and affirm each other daily (Heb. 3 v.13) keeping accountable to one another.

# Balancing Marriage and Ministry

- Can you teach in the Sunday school?
- Will you lead the prayer meeting?
- Can you take the youth group to the beach?
- We need you in the band!
- Don't forget to visit Jerry in hospital.
- You're on the church committee.
- The prayer walking team is waiting for you!

Most of us are involved in ministry of some sort or other through our Church. For some people this will be full-time, while for others it may be fitted around a busy working life/family life or home life.

Often ministry can take priority over our family, over everything else - so how do we keep the balance?

## What about Balance?

Balance is a word that we all use, often in optimism but rarely in reality. Those who have ever spent time balancing a set of kitchen scales know the time it takes often to get the balance right. Nowhere is this more difficult than in the area of marriage and ministry.

The pressures are different for those in full-time ministry and for those in demanding jobs or home life but both have the potential for high stress levels when the balance (that word again) goes awry.

The balance of keeping both ministry and marriage poised will need constant re-working and re-assessing, simply because both keep changing. Situations change, family grows, we get older, gifting develops, we move etc.

## Getting the balance right!

**The good news is however that we are given some great Biblical principles that will help us under-gird the balancing act.**

**Are there priorities? Ministry comes fourth in the order of biblical priorities, believe it or not. First in the biblical priorities' top ten is our personal relationship with the Lord - the first commandment is that we will *LOVE no other God. It's to be our no.1 priority whether married or not. Are we spending personal time with God alone?***

*Second comes the only key relationship God created right from the very first breath of human creation - marriage, Genesis 1 v.27. The relationship of marriage is unique simply because there is no one else who can be a husband to your wife (or vice versa).*

*Thirdly comes our relationship with our children - the biblical challenge of a parent's responsibilities are disciplining, teaching and caring for their children - it's over-whelming. We are the only mother our children have, and the only father. There are no substitutes.*

*Fourth comes the ministry or work God gives us to do.*

Although we may give theoretical assent to this order, usually the number of waking hours each day are consumed in the opposite order. For example, most of our time will be spent doing our job or ministry - maybe 8-10 hours a day. Then we'll spend 2 hours with our family, mostly round meal tables, one hour with our wives/ husbands - often much less than that; and maybe 15 minutes on our personal quiet time and our relationship with God.

The result is that the amount of time spent on each task each day actually dictates an opposite priority. It is inevitable that we will spend huge amounts of time on ministry and job, they need it, and less on a quiet time but this should not change the Biblical priorities we hold to.

## Where is God's emphasis?

As far as God is concerned He puts the emphasis on relationships, not work. The importance is not WHAT I DO for Him but WHO I AM for Him. Just reread that sentence to yourself.

Similarly it is not how I 'fix' things for my husband or wife or how much I earn but who I am as a husband/ wife. If I keep this principle in mind, I will see more clearly the way I can balance my attention to my husband/ wife and family and then in turn my attention to the ministry God has called me to - even though my ministry itself may be full of relationships. It will mean that I will ensure that my marriage and family relationships are good, BEFORE I work at my ministry relationships. Incidentally, that is why the Bible forbids ministry responsibility to a person who does not retain good family relationships, *1 Timothy 3 vs.1-13.*

## Is there a strategy?

Yes, put simply it is 'act in faith'! Analyze carefully whether you feel you have got the priorities right and the emphasis right in some of the ways you

*Take action, however drastic this may seem.*

balanced, or unbalanced, your marriage and ministry recently. Then take action, however drastic this may seem. This action must be taken 'in faith', believing that God will miraculously work out the details. The Holy Spirit is given to empower us to do this, *James 1 v.5* (wisdom).

None of this is to suggest that there are easy decisions to be made, speaking as a man now. Sometimes it is hard. Sometimes we have to do hard things for the sake of the gospel. There will be times when your wife will say good-bye to you as you leave for a ministry trip. She will smile and wave happily, but go in and cry as she seeks the miracles needed in the days you are away.

There will be other times when you will suddenly cancel a trip away knowing that you are letting down scores of people, or losing an excellent opportunity, but knowing that your wife or child needs you near home at this time. There are no easy answers. Be encouraged, even Paul in the New Testament had to make hard choices in this area.

## Spice it this week

Work through point three above and apply these 7 'balancing rules' to any decision you, make.

1. Pray together, husband and wife, daily.
2. Take a day off once a week (see the spice on 'a Sabbath rest').
3. Keep accountable to each other in time and place.
4. Keep promises you make to your family.
5. Recognise 'seasons' in your family life, i.e. when the normal routine is disturbed by for example a new baby, illness, exams, etc. and make allowances for this.
6. Delegate work and trust them to do it.
7. Remember that busyness is not godliness.

## Spice from the Word
*Mark 2 vs.27-28*

When we look at the ministry of Jesus we sometimes see all the action but miss the times when he rested and withdrew from the crowds.

When Jesus had this confrontation in the passage with the Pharisees he has just healed someone and they are up in arms that He had done this on a Sabbath day. Jesus turns around and answers them that the Sabbath day of rest was for the people not as a burden but as a day of healing and restoration, or rest and recuperation.

We need to look at the example of Jesus and be encouraged by his understanding of rest and time-out from 'ministry'. Our marriages can be a place of 'Sabbath rest' from the busyness of ministry.

When Jesus rested with his friends' he was more able to do the ministry he was called to do; that's his example for us to understand and enjoy.

# Covenant or Contract?

*The service was almost over. The large church was packed. In spite of the heat of mid-summer everyone was wearing their best silks and suits. Music, smiles, handshakes, laughter and the family followed as Kiran and Jema, holding hands, walked to the side aisle to sign the register. Declared legal, man and wife, Mr. and Mrs.* An agreement had been made by two parties to become one.

A contract was signed, or had they done more than that? What does this piece of paper really mean? Under a contract if one person fails to perform according to the contract, then the other party has no obligation to perform either and is no longer bound by the terms of the contract. Is this what we sign up for?

## A blood covenant

If we are biblical in our understanding of marriage, we sign up for a lot more than this. The biblical concept of marriage is that of a covenant. A blood covenant. Different from a contract in that it is totally independent of performance, and is irrevocable. The concept of a blood covenant in the Bible is the most enduring agreement possible. When men made such a covenant with each other it was commitment which said, 'all I have and all I am is yours, your enemies are my enemies and I am ready to give up even my life for you if need be.' Jonathan made such a covenant with David, Ruth with Naomi.

However, the most awesome covenant of all is that of Almighty God making a covenant with mankind. Committing all He is and all He has to us and demonstrating it powerfully, in the death and resurrection life of Jesus. An irrevocable covenant promise. As Jesus continues to be committed to us, covenanted to us, He says, 'I will never leave you or forsake you', *Hebrew 13 v.5 '*

## I'll keep my end of the bargain if you keep yours'

A marriage contract would say, 'I'll keep my end of the bargain, if you keep yours. If not I'll leave you and find someone else who'll make me happy.' For too many people that is their concept of marriage. In a marriage ceremony we say 'I will', a continuous verb meaning our promise will be continuous to each other.

Couples are caught in a cycle of fear of abandonment, insecurity, perfectionism and lack of trust, divorce and separations. This is not the Maker's intention when He designed marriage for us. It comes from Satan's lies. God's incredible intention is that our marriage is a reflection of His covenant relationship with us. That means I need to look closely at how Jesus relates to me to find

"I'll keep... if you keep...' A recipe for disaster'

out what my marriage covenant really is. It means I am totally committed to love and accept my husband or wife totally unconditionally. 'Till death do us part' is covenant language which says 'I am irrevocably committed to you until death separates us. My commitment to you has nothing to do with your achievements or performance. I have chosen you for life.'

---

*Mary sat in the garden, tears streaming down her face. 'This is too hard, too painful, I've got to get out of this marriage, surely God will understand, how can I forgive again and again?'*

*God gives us covenant for our blessing not for torture: he is there for us (Emmanuel), when it hurts too much, when it seems impossible. He's a God of possibilities but he gave us choice and whatever our choice he doesn't desert us. He sees the full picture, when we may have tunnel vision, just seeing the pain.*

*Gradually with the help of counseling Mary is being able to see God's covenant as the bigger picture and has written to her husband an understanding of the covenant they've made. She said, 'I choose today for our marriage not because I can trust you again but because I have chosen you forever.' Mary is recognizing she can not possibly do this without God's Holy Spirit enabling her every day to transform her attitude and turn something from being impossible to possible.*

**'I choose today for our marriage not because I can trust you again but because I have chosen you forever.'**

## Spice it up

Recognizing the power and seriousness of the covenant promise we have made to one another, watch out for 'contract attitude': 'If you don't do this, I'll do this'; 'I'll leave you'; 'go get a divorce if you like'. We must guard the covenant we have made. As you pray together this week ask the Holy Spirit to strengthen your commitment to that covenant promise. Go through your marriage vows together, putting in real life situations, remember the 'I WILL'.

## Spice from the Word
*Song of Songs 6 vs.1-12*

We all need friends who ask the right questions. As you look back on this incident through chapters 5 and 6, 'you will notice the important role played by friends in bringing lovers together again.

We should not pour out our marriage problems to everyone; however we should not be slow in getting help from trusted friends if we need it.

The friends do not rush in with loads of well meaning advice. They ask two important questions and in answering them, the girl solves her own problem.

There is a time and a place for such strong advice and often the right question can help more. Let us remember to apply this principle in marriage as well.

# Toxic Words

*Proverbs* is full of warnings about how we speak and use words: 'A gentle answer turns away wrath but a harsh toxic word stirs up anger.'

Do you know anyone whose words are kind and gracious most of the time - they could charm a cobra out of a hole - but then there is a tiny toxic arrow that spoils it all? Toxic arrow words just pop out of our mouths. Often unplanned, to us they may sound harmless. We forget them, but our partner who hears them doesn't. The task we have this week is to identify the arrows or 'toxic' words.

## Toxic Words

We have found the following list of toxic words helpful in identifying the arrows that stir up anger and give each other pain. They are partly adapted from, 'Words that Harm, Words that Heal'. T. Stafford.

---

### 1  Labelling
A subtle and very hurtful arrow.

'Stupid'

'Dumb'

'Hopeless'

These immediately put our partner down and are corrosive to love. If I turn to Rod and say, 'You're so insensitive', what can he do about it? Should he turn to me and to prove his sensitivity, burst into tears? Or if, in reply he says, 'You are so sensitive', it's disparaging and damning. We need to be aware of toxic labels.

---

### 2  Words that wear us down
These are words that leave us feeling tired and discouraged. 'Shut up', for example, is an abrupt and angry way to ask for quiet. For the same reason, swear words are an ugly, uncreative way of expressing feelings and leave a bad smell in a room.

---

## 3 Words that take out my partner's heart

Some words are devastating. Early on in our marriage, Rod and I agreed never to use the word 'divorce' in anger. It can turn a small argument into a death struggle. It breaks deep cracks into our love and commitment and can take out our partner's heart.

> *A few years ago, Rod and I had a strong disagreement. At the end of it Rod said to me, 'Ruthie, I feel so disappointed with you.' To Rod, that meant that I had saddened him, but to me it conveyed something far more painful.*
>
> *The word 'disappointed' conveyed fundamental disapproval that I couldn't change, a feeling that I was less than he wanted. As soon as I told Rod how I felt, he realized that it wasn't what he had meant at all; he was confining 'disappointed' to one small incident. But I had taken an arrow into my heart, feeling he was rejecting me. In love, Rod said how sorry he was and we have been careful not to use that phrase ever since.*

## 4 Words that overstate the point

When you are upset, it is easy to exaggerate. I am often guilty of this and my family delight in pointing it out to me!

'You are always late!'
'You never pick up dirty clothes!'

It simply isn't true. Nobody 'always' or 'never' does anything. These exaggeration arrows stop us getting our point across because they immediately cause defensiveness.

## 5 Words that rub salt in a wound

For a long time, Rod and I called a very dear friend of ours 'fat Prabhu' until we realized that he was very conscious of his portly shape and he wasn't really fat at all. We had offended him many times without realizing it. There may be other areas that it isn't loving to talk about, for example, old mistakes, old fights, or old failures. Teasing can be fun and gentle, but we have to be careful that it doesn't come poison-tipped.

The chart below of course simplifies things, and the examples are taken out of context and could be experienced in many different tones. But can you see how the 'toxic arrows' are so unhelpful and can damage our communication?

| Opening comment | Toxic Arrow | Understanding and helpful response |
|---|---|---|
| 'What a terrible day' | 'Don't bother telling me; you're always miserable' | 'Sounds like you're feeling shattered, it's been tough for you lately' |

| Opening comment | Toxic Arrow | Understanding and helpful response |
|---|---|---|
| 'Don't tell me you've spent all that money' | 'I'd like to see you doing better. I am trying you know' | 'Hey, you're angry about the way I spend money. Can we talk about it?' |
| 'Not tonight darling, I've got a headache' | 'You've always got a headache! What's wrong with you?' | 'Things must be awful; you've had a lot of tension lately (gives opportunity for speaker to admit to feelings about other things including sex).' |
| 'What am I going to do with this child?' | 'She's OK; it's you who is a rotten mother' | 'You're upset with her. What's the day been like? |

 ## Spice together this week

Read *James 1 vs.19-27* aloud together.

### Listening and Doing

[19]My dear brothers, take note of this: Everyone should be quick to listen, slow to speak and slow to become angry, [20]for man's anger does not bring about the righteous life that God desires. [21]Therefore, get rid of all moral filth and the evil that is so prevalent and humbly accept the word planted in you, which can save you.

[22]Do not merely listen to the word, and so deceive yourselves. Do what it says. [23]Anyone who listens to the word but does not do what it says is like a man who looks at his face in a mirror [24]and, after looking at himself, goes away and immediately forgets what he looks like. [25]But the man who looks intently into the perfect law that gives freedom, and continues to do this, not forgetting what he has heard, but doing it - he will be blessed in what he does.

[26]If anyone considers himself religious and yet does not keep a tight rein on his tongue, he deceives himself and his religion is worthless. [27]Religion that God our Father accepts as pure and faultless is this: to look after orphans and widows in their distress and to keep oneself from being polluted by the world.

- Pray for the Holy Spirit to 'bridle our tongues'. Once that toxic arrow is out of my mouth, I can't pull it back. We may need to ask forgiveness of one another right now.

- Honestly recollect some common 'toxic arrows' in your marriage.

- Decide together not to shoot them in the future.

- What phrases or words can be used instead?

 ## Spice from the Word
*Psalm 46 v.10*

'Be still and know that I am God.' Practice being still! Any time we are faced with conflict, anger flaring up, a biting reply on our lips - relax, listen to the still small inner voice of the Holy Spirit. The right words will come as we practise this, and rely more and more on inspiration.

# Overcoming Rejection

*'I wish you'd never been born',*
*'I'm too busy to bother with you now',*
*'You're hopeless'.*

Do any of those phrases sound familiar? Maybe you heard that or something similar when you were a child. All of us have a need for love and value. And all of us have been disappointed or hurt at some time because we did not get this in the way we needed. Some people can feel rejected because they believe they were unwanted. Perhaps later on at school or at home, parents or teachers preferred others to us and made it clear. 'Why aren't you like your brother?', 'You'll never make it' seem to ring in our ears. Even though actual words may have been said only once or twice, the power of those words is acute.

## Bonds of Rejection

As we grow up relatives or college friends may make comments about our appearance, 'she's so clumsy', 'he is just a computer geek'. We may have allowed even laughter and jokes about us in fun to become a cruel bond of rejection. There may have been circumstances which added to the rejection. Perhaps we were sent away to school because of difficulties at home, divorce or separation. In some families there is constantly a lack of praise and encouragement or excessive punishments for small mistakes.

The negative words and attitudes we have received can be used by Satan to imprison us. Rejection cannot be ignored and time does not 'heal'.

Rejection which is not faced up to and dealt with destroys our image of ourselves and others. The heart of rejection is not accepting ourselves as we are and wishing we were different. This affects how we behave towards one another, and so it can have devastating effects on us as a husband or wife. It can creep insidiously into every area of our marriage.

## Symptoms

When we are sick a doctor will look at the symptoms and treat the disease. Similarly we can recognise the symptoms of rejection and then open ourselves to the grace of God and His forgiving love as the very best Doctor to deal with the disease. Satan will try every means to trap us in rejection. He is a rejected being himself. Furthermore in *Genesis 3 vs. 23-24*, when Adam, our forefather, is forced to leave the Garden of Eden, he leaves ashamed and rejected. We are all born with his nature. The symptoms of suffering from rejection have been very helpfully observed by our friends Duncan and Vasanti Watkinson. They list:

1. **No real self worth**
   - Constantly undermining yourself
   - Hating yourself
   - Lacking in care or being over-concerned about appearance
   - Pre-conditioned to failure and disappointment
   - Wanting to opt out of life, staying in bed, suicidal thoughts

2. **Inadequate relationships**
   - Inability to give or receive love
   - Unable to make lasting relationships
   - Over-activity. Trying by achievements to gain acceptance
   - Difficulty in coming under any kind of authority
   - Inability to trust
   - Over-praising yourself

3. **Fear of rejection**
   - Dislike of going into a crowded room
   - Insecurity in conversations
   - Lack of confidence because of what others might think, excessive shyness, agreeing too quickly, integrating behavior…

4. **Rejection of others**
   - No close friends, keeping people at arm's length
   - Finding it hard to express physical love
   - Reacting angrily when people try to get close either to challenge or praise you

So again it is not difficult to see how rejection when not dealt with will affect every area of marriage. It is a distinctive tool Satan uses to prevent us from really enjoying each other the way God intends us to.

# Loosed from Rejection

Shyla grew up in a home where her father had to be constantly travelling. Whenever he came home she longed to run into his arms for a hug and reassurance. She never got it. He was often drunk and beat her mother and both Shyla and her sister were taken to a neighbor's house for protection. Shyla left home at sixteen, fell in love and by seventeen was married and pregnant. Unable to find any security in her marriage she became infatuated with her boss in the small office where she worked. Shyla was trapped, her husband discovered the affair and took the baby and threw her out the house. Her boss lost interest and sacked her. One night while staying with a friend she drank a bottle of highly toxic insecticide. She woke up in the hospital, angry to be alive.

Over the next few weeks her uncle and her aunt opened their home and their hearts to her. She began to be honest with herself and with them and to face squarely the symptoms of rejection and all the hurts in her life. They pointed her to *Isaiah 53 v.3* and shared that Jesus had borne our rejection, 'He was despised and rejected by men' for our sake. She painfully began to list memories of hurt. She then consciously invited Jesus into her life, to allow His grace to sweep into the inner recesses of her mind and spirit. It was as if the chains and handcuffs snapped off her arms as she repented. She was reminded of the truth

> ***She chose to forgive them and let go of the debt they owed her.***

of *1 Peter 1 v.18*, 'You were redeemed from the empty way of life handed down to you from your forefathers, with the blood of Jesus.' It was a slow and deep healing process. The day came when she asked the Lord to cleanse and forgive her for all the hatred towards her father, husband and men in general. She chose to forgive them and let go of the debt they owed her. There was a dramatic change in all her relationships, with everyone. She began to laugh, relax and reach out to people. She took interest in how she looked. Her whole body seemed to reflect the freedom inside. Her little daughter has a new mother. This is not the end the story. She is still working at reconciliation with her husband. Shyla's testimony is a wonderful tribute to the grace of God. Shyla is being transformed from the inside out since God's grace overcame rejection. He wants the same for you and me.

## Spice Together

Your story may not be as dramatic as Shyla's. Yet you may recognise the symptoms of rejection in your life. Remember that sometimes our partner sees this more clearly than we do and we may need to hear what they say. Walk together through these seven steps to overcoming rejection.

Seven steps to overcoming rejection

1. Honestly face up to any symptom of rejection and ask for the Grace of God to take you to victory.
2. List what has caused the hurts, this may take some time!
3. Read together *Isaiah 53 v.3*. Jesus has borne our sin and rejection. He was rejected for us.

4. The chains of rejection are broken only on the cross. *1 Peter 1 v.18*, 'You were redeemed from the empty way of life handed down to you from your forefathers, with the blood of Jesus'

5. Recognise that reacting in rejection is sin. Confess it to the Lord and ask for his forgiveness.

6. Forgive and release! All the people whom you remember having contributed to the feelings of rejection - name them and consciously release them from the debt of love they owe to you. Jesus taught us to pray, 'forgive us our debts as we forgive our debtors'

7. Choose a new way of thinking each day. As you wake up say, 'I am a son / daughter of the King' by God's grace. Endeavour to pass this acceptance on to one another and to others, especially your children.

### Spice from the Word
*1 John 3 v.1*

This is a verse to meditate on. Take time to look up this verse in as many different Bible translations as you have. 'How great is the love the Father has lavished on us that we should be called children of God'. Think - Who am I? - in light of this verse.

# Praise Pictures

*Right in the middle of the Bible is a unique marriage manual, Song of Songs. This romantic love poem paints a beautiful story of how expressions of love can turn an attractive but insecure bride, who says about herself, 'I am black, but lovely… do not stare at me, my mother's sons were angry with me; they made me caretaker of the vineyards', (1 vs.5-6), into a person with confidence, glowing with a sense of beauty and worth, (2 v.1), 'I am a rose of Sharon, a lily of the valley.'*

That's incredible! Well, how does this happen? King Solomon, her young husband, has the key. He paints beautiful praise pictures to give her vivid illustrations of how precious and wonderful she is. One example is chapter 1 v.9, 'To me, my darling, you are like my mare among the chariots of Pharaoh.' Not many brides would like to be called a horse! But here is the difference; it's the picture which comes to her mind as he says these words. She would have known about the mighty stallions, black, brown, or piebald, fighting that pulled the Egyptian army chariots. But most importantly, she would also know that just one, a unique pure white mare, was specially chosen before all the others to pull Pharaoh's chariot. Do you get the picture through her eyes? She sees it as 'I am unique, outstanding, the only one to you.'

**A unique pure white mare**

*Every marriage needs a daily dose of praise. Look for the best in your loved one today and start capturing it in a picture he or she can mentally see, understand and relate to.*

## 'He's got muscles of Iron'

For seven years we lived at Mahabalipuram on the east coast. Every night the lighthouse beamed out a steady stream of light every nine seconds. Listed on the nautical chart, its position and place can be identified, unchanging. When I say to Rod, 'Love, you are like a beam of light to me, just like the lighthouse. I feel so secure in your unchanging care for me and the family', in Rod's mind he sees the rock-solid lighthouse and recognizes that I'm telling him he is a pillar of strength to me. Every time he sees a lighthouse or catches a beam of light, he is reminded by the symbol of my genuine love and appreciation of him. We become secure in one another's love. *Song of Songs 6 v.3*, 'I am my beloved's and my beloved is mine.'

You may be thinking, 'But I'm not very imaginative, I can't think in these kinds of ways.' We don't need to be an expert copywriter or artist. All of us have said things like, 'She's a star' and 'he's got muscles of iron' and 'his eyes glow like coal'. We need to take the trouble to pick up on pictures, symbols and events around our own marriage and home that our loved one can identify with.

## 'Oh this old dress'

Many of us are so unused to receiving praise that we try to bat it off, 'No, I'm not like that' or 'Don't be ridiculous' and although we ache for the self-worth and value that praise rather than flattery gives, we seem to reject it. We might react clumsily out of embarrassment. Imagine a husband trying a picture of praise...

He (smiling), 'In that dress you look like a freshly picked rose'

She (frowning), 'Oh this old dress'

He (thinking), She didn't like that, I've said the wrong thing. I'd better keep quiet.

She (upset) He doesn't give me compliments anymore, whatever I look like.

He (thinking gloomily) Now what's her problem?

We can wound one another by a flippant reaction or we may just toss aside the praise. It is just as important that we learn how to receive praise as well as give it!

*Important that we learn how to receive praise as well as give it!*

Throughout the Bible the Lord reminds His people in powerful praise pictures of how precious they are to Him and wants them to hear and respond as David does when he replies to the Lord, 'You are my rock and my hiding place.'

So if your loved one practises these pictures with/on? you, receive them. 'I'm so happy that you told me that' or 'that's so loving of you to tell me, it makes me feel great'. In this way the giver also receives the glow of reflected praise.

## Spice it up

Read though Songs of Songs highlighting the praise pictures (there are over 40 of them!) Look around your locality, home and into memories for opportunities to give praise pictures to your beloved.

Another suggestion, write them down in a small note under her pillow, in his briefcase, in her Bible, on his desk, in her handbag, the places are endless.

## Spice from the Word
*Song of Songs 5 vs.9-16*

Her friends find the distressed bride and ask her a good question. They point her thoughts away from herself and her trouble, to her husband's outstanding character. She replies with a glowing description of her beloved. It is the only detailed picture of the man in the whole song. The aim of husbands should be to be worthy of such admiration. In Christ it is possible.

# In-laws or Outlaws!

> 'Hey, have you heard this one?' asked Raj on hearing that I'd recently become a mother-in-law.
>
> 'What's the definition of mixed emotions?'
>
> 'Can't think,' I replied.
>
> 'When your brand new Toyota disappears over the cliff with your mother-in-law in the back seat!'
>
> Raj ducked as I threw a well-aimed cushion at him!

*Why do mother-in-laws always get such a bad press? What is it that creeps so insidiously into our extended family relationships that causes so much stress?* One thing we have noticed, and constantly pray and work at rooting out, is a competitive spirit. Trying to battle for the top place in the affection of one another. Mothers with their sons and fathers with their daughters are particularly vulnerable here.

## Intimate Separateness

In the chapter 'Leaving and Cleaving' we looked at spices to strengthen our togetherness as husband and wife and that is the first essential factor in coping with in-laws. If we ourselves work at building a firm reliable relationship with each other we are far more likely to be able to cope with the strain of in-laws.

Vasanth and Praneetha, in Visag, describe their journey in discovering the wonderfully secure experience of family togetherness with their extended family while keeping their own unique 'intimate separateness'.

Look at some of the suggestions they have worked through with their in-laws so as to keep loving and honouring them right on throughout our marriage.

## Seven Ideas for Loving your In-laws!

**1. Signal support:** We need to keep showing and demonstrating our oneness with our wives and husbands in front of our in-laws. Complimenting how your wife looks, or commenting on your husband's abilities are all ways of signaling your oneness. Even standing or sitting alongside each other while talking in the family circle, are all signals to your parents and other family members that you are one

*If we ourselves work at building a firm reliable relationship with each other we are far more likely to be able to cope with the strain of in-laws.*

**2. Avoid Debt:** In every way try and avoid being in debt financially to your in-laws. If you have to borrow, take from a friend or from a bank etc, rather than from your parents-in-law. Finances always - however loving you are - bring strain. A gift from parents, as long as it is given freely and not as an attempt to bind you, is usually not a problem, but a debt will put you under such obligation, that you will find a normal loving relationship difficult.

**3. Take advice but...:** Parents-in-law love to feel needed, and we should ask and take advice from them. But it is important that you are seen to be making decisions together and independently of them. One of you may feel intimidated by one or other of your parents, and may not feel able to raise an opinion in front of them, and so it is important to decide together beforehand, and then tell your parents what you have decided, and thank them for their help.

**4. Space Alone:** This is essential if you are living in the same house. Take opportunities to go for a daily stroll alone together, or claim a balcony as being your own or a corner of the terrace, and set aside an hour when you can just share the things that are concerning you. This can be a life-line for a wife who otherwise may be living in her mother-in-law's house, and has no other time to just talk to you. There need not be a problem that has to be sorted out; it just needs to be time when you can re-assert your oneness as a couple.

**5. Be Friends!** Make sure that there are times of relaxation and fun together with in-laws, rather than just times of work, cooking, housework

'Being Friends!'

etc. This is particularly important if you are living together in the same house. Make sure some of your outings are inclusive of all. It is a balance between the point above and this one that will make a happy in-law household. Pray that your relationship will make a mother-in-law into a 'mother-in-grace'!

**6.   Visit Together:** If you are both present all the time with both your sets of in-laws, there will be less chance of misunderstandings arising from remarks that may be said in your absence. Obviously this is impossible when you are living in the same house, but it can save a lot of heartache when you are living in a separate house. Perhaps you will be giving financial support to one or both sets of parents.

> You may give by internet banking but we have friends who always go together to hand over their monthly cheque, always make a point of ensuring that the wife hands the cheque to the husband's parents, and the husband hands the cheque to the wife's parents. This is just a small thing that signals strongly to both sets of parents that it is not just a son or a daughter who is supporting them, but it is both supporting both. This little practice has brought much healing to an otherwise very hurtful in-law problem.

**7.   Keep Needing them:** There will always be a danger that we will swing too far one way or the other - either too much in the pockets of our in-laws, or too separate. They need to feel needed, and we need them. There are obvious ways we can do this – especially with children, and grandparents are a. wonderful source of baby sitters! But they need to feel needed in other ways too giving practical help, giving advice, being there in crises, a shoulder to cry on, an ear to listen. Some of us are blessed with having in-laws who are great friends. But it doesn't usually come easily. Friendships and supportive relationships need cultivating and building. Let's strive towards making our in-laws our best friends.

## A word in a mother-in-law's ear...

I have a wonderful son in law Joe, the best daughters-in-law anyone could ask for Kirti, Shiyani, and Michelle, who are becoming my special friends. When our eldest son Luke was getting married I asked my own wise sister-in-law (herself a mother-in-law of three), 'What tips can you give me for being a good mother-in-law Ro?' She said to me, very simply, 'Ruthie, lay down any right you think you might have, especially the right to take offence or be hurt. Look always for their good, not your own.'

Powerful words – reflective of this Spice from the Word.

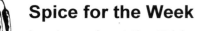

## Spice for the Week

Look again at the 7 ideas. Choose one to work at this week. Spend a few moments now praying for your parents, thanking God for them, and listening to the prompting of the Holy Spirit as He guides you into right attitudes.

## Spice from the Word

*Col 3 vs.1-14 - Consider what we should 'put off' and 'put on'*

'**Put off** anger, rage, malice and slander and filthy language from your lips. Do not lie to one another, since you have taken off your old self.'

'**Put on** (v.12) compassion, kindness, humility, gentleness and patience. Bear with each other, and forgive whatever you may have against one another...'

# Budgeting

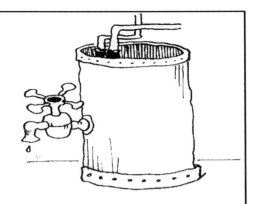

## The Water Tank

Of all the gifts that God holds us accountable for, money is the most tangible and measurable. The way we budget and use money will reflect the way we use our

and more important God. So with this in mind, let's review the way we use the bigger intangible gifts of money.

One of the best talks I have heard given on family budgeting, was given by Maggie and Roop Singh at a Cornerstone House seminar, where they illustrated their talk with the idea of a water tank. Your income is like the inflow of supply into the tank, and the outflow is the expenditure. The idea of the family budget is to ensure that there is always enough water in the tank to meet the demands of the outflow.

Financial problems in a family can come about in a few common ways:

a) There is insufficient control of the Outlet Tap - When we talk about money, we talk about the top of the tank, not the bottom. We say 'not enough income'; 'pay is too little'; 'we need a second or third income to survive'. We should be focusing on the Outlet Tap - the expenses. The problem is that we don't like to admit that there could be things we could do without or even should wait for.

b) Credit is becoming increasingly easy - When we buy on credit, it is like trying to take water out of an already dry tank. The income is not coming fast enough to keep balance in the tank. Credit companies are quick to exploit our desire for 'buy now, pay later'. The problem is that our expenses inevitably go up but a corresponding increase in our income is not guaranteed. We constantly worry. It only takes a sudden, unexpected break in the supply (illness, loss of job, transfer, etc...), for us to face financial bills we cannot possibly pay. This is devastating.

c) <u>Two tanks for two incomes:</u> These days, when many families will have both husband and wife earning, there can be an attitude that leads to competition, jealousy, and suspicion; and it leads to blame when problems arise. A couple, no matter what their salaries, must have a common tank into which they both pour. It is only then that you can share proper responsibility in using resources God has given your family.

## How should we budget?

Budgeting is like deciding how many pipes lead in at the top of the tank, and how many lead out and how big each pipe ought to be. It affects the speed of water flow through each pipe (as cash flows). Work a monthly budget rather than a yearly one. It is easier to keep track of this.

First, estimate your total income per month. Do not 'assume bonuses and extras. Calculate only for what you know is your regular income. Then, write in your fixed expenditure - rent, loan repayments, PF, tithes and offering, school fees etc... If you decide to write in, as fixed expenditure, a regular amount put aside for saving, however small, you will be able to reap untold benefits.

Only after you have accumulated the fixed expenditures, should you calculate the other expenses, dealing first with food provisions, gas, electricity, travel and other necessities. Then deal with clothing, entertainment and holidays.

It is then a good idea to have a bit of extra expenditure, which will enter your budget, and remember; a review of your budget is essential. Review this after six months.

## Don't fall into the trap of thinking...

- ...'I like what you've bought. I want it too.'

- ...'its no problem if I fall behind in payments just for a couple of months.'

- ...'things are OK now in my finances, so I don't need to bother praying so much about it.'

- ...'Just for this month I will use my tithe for other pressing expenses'

## Spice it up

- Make a list of all your expenses in a month. Be brutal in deciding how you can cut down some expenses where it is possible. Some starter questions for a healthy budget... Can we...

Less fast food?

Repair old, don't buy new?

Wait until next month?

The same, but a cheaper brand?

Review the credit and loans you presently have. You have to tell each other of any bills outstanding – even if it's a small one

- If you haven't already budgeted, write a monthly budget this week.
- Discuss together your long-term financial plans and goals.

## Spice from the Word
*Ecclesiastes 5 v.10 and vs.18-20 and 1 Timothy 6 v.10*

We can often get weighed down by our money and feel guilty for having it or anxious about not having enough.

In *Ecclesiastes* we read that money will never satisfy like God can (verse 10). Later in the same chapter (verses 18-20), we see how we are encouraged to enjoy money that we earn. Read those verses again. God gives us good things like money to enjoy and we mustn't let it become a burden to us.

In *1 Timothy 6 v.10* we are told that it is LOVE of money that is the root of all evil, not money itself. So be encouraged to enjoy what God has given you, whether a small amount or large and don't let it rule your life.

# Danger Zones

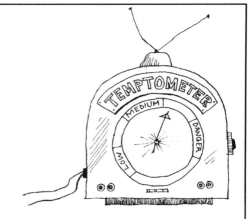

**'I'd never have an affair' is one of the most dangerous statements we can make. We are all vulnerable.** In fact when we look at David's affair with Bathsheba, we realize that no one, however chosen, gifted or powerfully used by God is immune from temptation. As believers in God's word we know and we are all committed to what God says about adultery and how he hates divorce and yet even this knowledge is not stopping the escalation of affairs amongst committed Christians. Our goal this week is to take a clear look at the process and the behavioral patterns that lead us into an affair. Forewarned is forearmed - beware of the danger zones. The following progress of a typical affair is adapted from 'Broken Promises' (Dr Henry Virkler).

## How did it happen?

Meet Suja and Ashin, a creative, talented couple both in their early thirties; they have been married six years.

| Suja's perspective | Ashin's perspective |
|---|---|
| Suja is lonely, has low self-esteem and reaches out for emotional support and affection. | Ashin is busy in business, highly competitive and satisfied. Loves Suja but is too tired at the end of a day to 'carry' her emotionally. |
| Suja is frustrated and angry, nags Ashin and blames him for lack of involvement at home. | Ashin, still over-committed at work tries to help Suja, makes a few attempts but falls back to old patterns.  |

| Suja's perspective | Ashin's perspective |
|---|---|
| Suja is vulnerable. A casual introduction at church to a friend's husband leads to fantasies. He always seems so concerned and compassionate. She spends increasing amounts of time at the friend's house. His wife often has to go away looking after her own parents. Innocent touching begins. | Ashin's mind is elsewhere. Although he loves Suja and the children, he has no idea of the blossoming relationship. |
| Suja feels guilty yet excited as the relationship heats up. The affair is not a sudden thing. Secret meetings are planned. Close friends at church begin to suspect something. Suja rationalizes her relationship, 'If it feels good, God must want us for each other' 'It's not adultery, we haven't slept together'. | Ashin is still not aware of any unfaithfulness. He's quite grateful for a lessened demand for her attention and is pleased that she seems to be taking more interest in her appearance. |
| Finally it happens. A sexual experience, fear, raw passion, guilt and a lot of secret meetings. She covers her tracks with lies and rationalizes what is happening. She acts the faithful wife at church, which is stressful. So Bible reading and church attendance become less frequent. No sexual interest in Ashin. | Ashin is confused and beginning to worry about Suja. A friend tells him of his suspicions. He knows intuitively that something is wrong, but is afraid to face the truth. |

## Danger Zone - Orange! Warning

*What is seen here in the lives of Suja and Ashin is that temptation to sexual sin most often starts with unfulfilled emotional needs.* This is why we as Christians become so vulnerable. We are called to love one another, support each other and pray for one another. A Christian friendship may certainly be instrumental in helping someone through a difficult situation. Both people's self-esteem is built up and what seems depressing and hopeless now sparkles with newfound energy and life. 'It all seems so right.' Satan is very successful at mixing good with evil. He did it from the beginning. Read *Genesis 31 v.6*. As we close our eyes to God's instructions **Flirting is out** of absolute faithfulness, we see relationships through a distorted lens and move more deeply into sin. Proverbs warns us strongly about wrong friendships. Flirting is out, *Proverbs 6 v.25*. We need to watch our words, *Proverbs 2 v.16; 5 v.3*.

## Danger zone - Red Alert! Affairs of the mind

As Suja began to allow fantasies to take hold in her mind, her thoughts became uncontrolled.

Jesus talks about this in *Matthew 5 v.28*. Out of the heart the mouth speaks. Jesus spoke radically. You think you can fantasise, dream and wish for your partner to be like 'someone else'? That is an affair of the mind. Lusting after someone in your mind is as sinful as adultery. Jesus made that clear. There is no room for any compromise. There are subtle ways of entering this danger zone; mostly done in secret, such as browsing the internet for pornographic web sites. This can be in pictorial or written form. Pornography of all kinds turns sex into an animal encounter dehumanizing people. A man may claim that this will stimulate him sexually for his wife, but it has no power to promote love or compatibility. The key to that is only in passionate, sacrificial serving love for his wife. Such wonderful love cannot grow while the mind is committing adultery induced by pornography, however stimulating.

## Danger Zone - Flashing Signals! The drip feed

Watch what we watch! Multi-media streams into our homes which can drip feed attitudes that work against our loving commitment to each other. For example, 'soaps' slowly drip feed us into believing that 'it's not wrong, is it?' Suja spent hours watching her two favorite soaps, which were full of affairs and infidelity. Gradually she became insecure, feeling that an affair might one day be inevitable in her own marriage.

The drip-feed effect of the programmes meant that she lost sight of God's hold on her marriage to Ashin, worrying unnecessarily that he would abandon her. She soon recognized that the root of the problem was the amount of time she was watching television programmes. She said 'You know, I prayed about it and God just helped me break the habit; basically I saw God's protection over our marriage and all the good things again instead of the rot'.

> *The drip-feed effect of the programmes meant that she lost sight of God's hold on her marriage*

If you ever find that the unbelievable is happening and a third person is intruding into your marriage or you're in the danger zone, act fast. Love is tough. **You are in an exclusive covenant relationship, which is the most precious in the world**. Confront strongly. Sometimes the 'bucket of cold water' treatment is what we need to shake us back into reality and be aware of a danger. It is never a Christian attitude to be 'understanding' of your partner if he or she becomes infatuated with someone else.

## Spice it up

Write a love letter to your beloved, expressing your commitment and faithfulness. Describe to him / her as fully as you can, your affirmation of the unique treasure God has given you in them. Use as many 'feeling' words as you can!

## Spice from the Word
*Proverbs 3 vs.5-8*

'I can handle it'. The shift from reliance on ourselves to admission of our own powerlessness is often long and tough. The reality is that when faced with sexual temptation, we need help. As we admit our powerlessness the magnificent power of God is displayed and is one of strength.

# Introvert or Extrovert?

## Opposites attract!

Whatever your cultural background-Whether our marriage was 'arranged' by family or friends- or a 'love match', we may have found that our personalities are very different. In fact, in many arranged marriages, parents or pastors deliberately look for a life partner who complements us.

Last night I was listening to Asha about a recent internet proposal she had had. 'He's very confident and strong minded. He wants to be independent and enjoy his two years abroad. I think he'll complement me. I'm really timid when it comes to meeting new people.' We talked in depth about how opposites challenge, enrich and fascinate one another, but the fascinations later on in marriage can turn to frustration and hurt.

'You don't make sense'
'Why aren't you normal like me?'

We can even come to the conclusion that we are totally incompatible. We've married the wrong person. The wonder is that marriage compatibility is created, rather than given as a ready-wrapped instant package on our wedding day.

## Personality preferences

*There always comes a stage when we recognise that we are both two very different personalities with very different pasts.* Not only are we born looking different, but with preferences towards different types of thinking and acting. Struggles can come when we don't recognise this. It may help you to do a simple personality test, good websites are available for this.

Take Lena and Vishram who have been married for five years and have two children. Vishram is a highly motivated junior executive. Lena worked as a nurse before they were married. Now she sometimes does night shifts but is usually at home with the children. Their marriage was arranged by their church pastor who felt they would complement one another, with both families in full agreement. Vishram is an outgoing extrovert, easy going and friendly, ready to eagerly join in any activities, good at grasping things and making things happen. He loves his work with people and has a great deal of involvement in the outreach and youth work at church.

*a 'kilometer wide and a centimeter deep'.*

Lena is quite an introvert, yet nevertheless is warm, gentle with people, very conscientious and dependable. Lena is often asked to do administrative work behind the scenes at work. She has strong ideas of her own and thinks issues through before she speaks. Vishram told us that after they were married, Lena's aura of depth and reliability and her organizational skills fascinated him. But now five years into their marriage, he is finding her too quiet and too sensible.

*'I signed my life away to an ice-berg.'*

'Oh Leena's the shy type; not my sort at all.'

She seemed to have no sense of humour, was fussy, and not willing to have the home full of the youth that he wanted. Lena at first had admired and been proud of Vishram as he was always the life and soul of the party, but now she felt that he was a 'kilometer wide and a centimeter deep'. She felt hurt as he tried to push her into up-front ministry with the youth. Her sense of rejection was intensified when he said one day 'I signed my life away to an ice-berg.'

## It's OK to be different

All Lena wanted to do was go home to her own family who understood her and her quiet ordered household that she loved. It was at this point that they asked for help.

'...creative support...'

During counseling, they discovered how their temperaments were so different. They had been trying to force their preferences on each other. Both were amazed that they could be right, normal, acceptable, and Godly, while expressing things so differently. Vishram began to realize that while he could initiate ideas with the youth to stimulate spiritual growth and thinking, Lena could creatively support him and plan intricately how it could work in practice. Vishram grew to love the peace and quiet that Lena created at home compared to the noise and bustle of the office and meetings. Instead of forcing her to keep an open home, he supported her in spending time enjoying their own children together in the evenings. Lena also began to develop her social skills by joining Vishram each Saturday night for the coffee house outreach. Vishram was willing to visit her family more often. God has made us unique and different. In accepting one another under His Spirit's control, our different temperaments become complementary.

**Instead of forcing her...**
**...he supported her**

## Spice for this week

There are many interesting websites which give personality profile testing. For example, www.humanmetrics.com is a good place to start. Try one together this week. Look at the analysis to help to understand each other's strengths and weaknesses.

## Spice from the Word
*2 Corinthians 12 vs.9-10*

When we know that we are loved, accepted and approved by God, it transforms our attitudes about how we see ourselves. In fact Paul says here that his weaknesses (maybe physical or characteristic traits he did not like much) actually gave more opportunity for Jesus' power and grace to be evident in his life. Incredible as it seems, when we are weak in ourselves, we are then strong in the empowering grace of our Lord Jesus Christ.

# Who doesn't like chocolate?

*Did you know that research has shown that the reason why some of us love chocolate is that it stimulates the release of pleasurable chemicals into our bloodstream, similar to the feelings of being 'in love'!?*

Ruthie travelled abroad last year and as usual brought back some exciting sweets, soaps and perfumes. Digging around in this bag of goodies I came across a tube of 'chocolate body paint'. 'That would be fun for our five year-old', I thought, 'to paint a picture on his arm and then lick it off'. To my amazement, I discovered that Ruthie hadn't bought it for that reason; it was 'for us' she said mysteriously.

## Without shame attached

But it also raises the question as to what is and what isn't permissible in our sexual enjoyment of each other's bodies. In the Prayer Book readings for the year, the Old Testament passage on marriage is from *Genesis chapter 2*. It stops one verse short of the end of the chapter, missing out that most revealing - verse 25 'The man and his wife were both naked and they felt no shame'. Why did the selectors feel that such a verse was inappropriate for public reading? Could

> **'The man and his wife were both naked and they felt no shame'.**

it be because Satan has so twisted the concept of sex, that in our minds it becomes something totally shameful, only done in the dark, and an act from which God probably turns His face? Of course the opposite is true - sexual love in marriage should have no shame attached to it. We can be totally guiltless revelling in each other's bodies, and in an act which God both invented and commanded us to do, *Genesis 1 v.28*. Paul advocates no restrictions on our sexual enjoyment in marriage, except for short periods of specific prayers, *1 Corinthians 7 vs.3-5*.

## Is it right?

Some questions we are asked regularly are these: How far can we go? Is oral sex permissible? Can we stimulate ourselves with pictures, films or material from the Internet? What about aids to sexual stimulation? We believe that there are two clear guiding Biblical principles which we should focus on.

### What is mutually loving and acceptable to one another?

Sexual enjoyment is a shared enjoyment between the two of you. There may be some sexual activities which one of you cannot enjoy for some reason. Sadly, many of us have experienced sexual abuse before we were married - in our childhood or youth. Our subconscious may be deeply scarred and needs the understanding patience and love of our husband or wife. The good news is that our Father, who gives His children gifts, has given us exquisite physical intimacy as a wedding gift. This is to bring healing and wholeness into areas of our lives which may have been damaged; to bring the joy of total belonging and restoration. We need to be understanding of one another and if our partner does not enjoy an area of sexual activity, we are to respect that - but gently look for an opportunity to talk and pray together about it.

*Exquisite physical intimacy as a wedding gift.*

### Is a third party entering your sexual life?

By this we mean any other person's involvement in our sexual life. Thus pictures of others in sexual poses to stimulate can never be right. 'Can a man walk on hot coals without his feet being burned?' *Proverbs 6 vs.27-28.* This is written in the context of 'lusting in your heart', in your emotions, thought-life and fantasies. Similarly, no sexual fantasy of someone else, which we may put into our minds while making love, can be excused as an aid to making love. By the same token, masturbating, where we fantasise by ourselves about anyone other than our beloved, will only frustrate and lead to sexual sin. God's pattern in our sexual revelling must be between the two of us alone, so if you can get hold of some chocolate body paint - and you are both happy about it, go for it! The Lord will laugh with you!

 **Spice for this week**

- Read together aloud the following passage from *Song of Songs chapter 7 (from The Message)*, taking the role of Lover and Beloved.

- Try something different and enjoy it!

Exquisite physical intimacy as a wedding gift.

## Song of Solomon 7

[1]Shapely and graceful your sandaled feet, and queenly your movement
Your limbs are lithe and elegant, the work of a master artist.
[2]Your body is a chalice, wine-filled.
Your skin is silken and tawny like a field of wheat touched by the breeze.
[3]Your breasts are like fawns, twins of a gazelle.
[4]Your neck is carved ivory, curved and slender.
Your eyes are wells of light, deep with mystery. Quintessentially feminine!
Your profile turns all heads, commanding attention.
[5]The feelings I get when I see the high mountain ranges
- stirrings of desire, longings for the heights
Remind me of you, and I'm spoiled for anyone else!
[6]Your beauty, within and without, is absolute, dear lover, close companion.
[7]You are tall and supple, like the palm tree,
and your full breasts are like sweet clusters of dates.
[8]I say, 'I'm going to climb that palm tree! I'm going to caress its fruit!'
Oh yes! Your breasts will be clusters of sweet fruit to me,
Your breath, clean and cool like fresh mint,
[9]your tongue and lips like the best wine.
Yes, and yours are, too - my love's kisses flow from his lips to mine.

*The Woman*
[10]I am my lover's. I'm all he wants. I'm all the world to him!
[11]Come, dear lover- let's tramp through the countryside.
[12]Let's sleep at some wayside inn, then rise early and listen to bird-song.
Let's look for wildflowers in bloom, blackberry bushes blossoming white,
Fruit trees festooned with cascading flowers.
And there I'll give myself to you, my love to your love!
[13]Love-apples drench us with fragrance, fertility surrounds, suffuses us,
Fruits fresh and preserved that I've kept and saved just for you, my love.

---

### Spice from the Word
*Song of Songs 1 vs.1-11:*

Study verse 2, contrast the kiss of the lover here with other kisses in the Bible, mentioned in

| | |
|---|---|
| - *Luke 7 v.45* | Find the kisses of commitment, friendship, |
| - *Luke 22 v.48* | forgiveness, admonition, or service. These |
| - *Luke 15 v.20* | should characterise our marriages. |
| - *1 Corinthians 15 v.20* | The deadly kiss of betrayal or flattery should |
| - *1 Samuel 20 v.41* | never enter our relationships. |

# Accepting one another into transparency

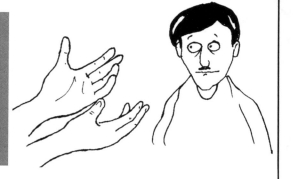

*How much can I dare to let you know about me? Will you accept me as I am, will you reject me? Questions we have asked secretly or openly.* Recently we sat quietly with a young couple listening to them daring to be really transparent with each other. The husband has come through deep hurt and sexual abuse as a child, which affected his attitude towards his wife. The fear burnt in his eyes as he said, 'If you condemn me for what I tell you or use this against me, I will never want to see you again.'

**Becoming vulnerable.** The cloak of silence, darkness or wrapping up the past sometimes seems safer to us than committing ourselves to being vulnerable to rejection or misunderstanding. A key element in growing into transparency and oneness, daring to be vulnerable, is communicating a constant feeling of acceptance to my husband or wife.

After spending some time with them we left and watched at a distance as they walked slowly towards the beach, the setting sun lightly glowing in their hair. As they returned, an hour or so later, the tired, tense lines on his face were now relaxed. After listening to the memories and hurt of her husband, it was vividly clear that his wife accepted him totally. The haunted look of fear was gone, and when asked how she felt, she simply said 'It just makes me love and respect him more for what God is doing in his life in spite of everything.' Instead of living with a painful guilty secret his frank openness had removed the power of accusation and guilt about his sexuality. Acceptance is a key theme of the gospel of Jesus.

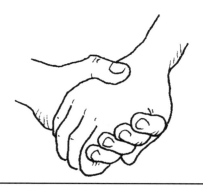

*Romans 15 v.7* - accept one another just as Christ accepted us.
*Romans 5 v.8* - Christ accepts us as we are and (Romans 8 v.1) removes condemnation.
*Hebrews 4 v.16* - we can feel free to approach Him without fear.

How often in our marriage we want each other to be almost perfect and when we begin to share our real fears about money, sex or our past we sense rejection, shut out and hurt. We need to learn to communicate a sense of understanding, warmth and closeness, acceptance, reflecting Jesus Himself, to our partners.

**Sharing the hidden me**

Yesterday I sat down on the bed next to Rod, looked at him and said, 'I'm afraid, can I tell you why?' He put his arm around me and listened as I listed the areas, some quite well hidden, of fear in my life. I was afraid of 'unknowns' in the future, afraid that illness would strike again, afraid of not being able to cope with all that had to be done through the hot weather, the list went on; Rod listened. I knew that a lot of my fear was groundless and irrational but as I became vulnerable and shared it, the gnawing ache in my stomach eased and I relaxed. Rod listened and recognized several physical needs and spiritual attacks that he gently and clearly pointed out to me, but above all he accepted my honest feelings as being valuable and real.

When our partner begins to share honest feelings with us we have a choice.

We can prevent transparency by our:

Advise
'Maybe you should…?'
'If you just do…?'

Ignorance
'Hey, there's no need to feel…?'
'I don't understand why you feel…?'

Attack
'Now stop being so…?'
'Maybe I was wrong, but you are so…?'

We can encourage transparency by:

Exploring
'When else do you feel like this…?'
'Tell me a bit more about…?'

Clarifying
'Are you saying that…?'
'Can you see where this may be coming from…?'

Emphasizing
'You really felt… did you also feel…?'
'If I were in your shoes I might feel.., do you feel like that?'

 **Spice it Together**

Take a few minutes for a bible check-up on growing into transparency.
Look up:
*Romans 15 v.7*
Why should we accept each other unconditionally?
*Romans 8 v.1*
In the light of this verse how should we feel?
*Hebrews 4 v.16*
How can I model this attitude to you?

 **Spice from the Word**
*1 Corinthians 11 v.28*

'But let a man (woman) examine himself.' Looking through our past can sometimes be like sifting through garbage. Resentments, fears or habits may have been built up over years. We need Jesus to clear away the rubbish, fill us daily with His love and strength. Confession should be a time of celebration knowing that through the cross we are forgiven, loved and accepted. Consider *Psalm 139 vs.23*, 24 as a prayer for you both.

# Intruders

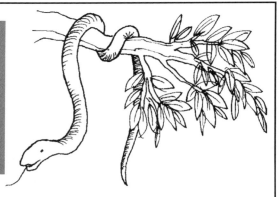

*The word 'intruder' seems to me to be a very menacing word, a word with a warning attached to it.*

I looked the word up in the dictionary and this is what it said:

**Intrude** - enter uninvited, thrust oneself (upon), force into or open.

**Intruder** - encroachment.

It's not a very nice description, is it? An intruder is definitely someone or something to beware of.

## The First Intruder

In the Bible, the first picture we have of married life is Adam and Eve alone in the beautiful garden God had created for them. They were together, and different in their togetherness from everything else in the Garden. God looked at them and he was delighted. But then an intruder, the serpent, slithers in between them and causes havoc, disobedience, isolation and separation from God and also destroys the perfect togetherness that Adam and Eve had before. We need to be alert to intruders.

## The Triangle

*An important thing to note here is that God is not an intruder. He is the centre of a marriage. A good picture to use to illustrate this is a triangle with God at the top, and the husband and wife either side of the bottom of the triangle. As the couple move closer towards God, so they become closer to each other.*

*In Ecclesiastes 4 vs.9-12 we have the picture of marriage as a three-stranded rope; God, husband and wife sewn together, a strong and unbreakable union.*

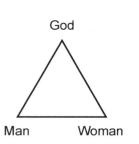

God

Man    Woman

## So who or what is an intruder?

David and Sheena lived a busy life; they had been married for over a year now and had got into a routine. Strong in their love for each other and their faith, they relied on these as a basis for everything else they did. Sheena knew David loved her even if she was out at meetings every night of the week and didn't get a chance to talk to him. David knew that Sheena would always be there for him even though he'd started to watch cricket much more often now with his friends. Slowly their lives got busier and they became more complacent with each other and in their relationship with God.

Sheena found herself talking late into the night after the meetings to a friend of David's, who was also there.

'It can't happen to us; he's the pastor.'

Sheena enjoyed his company, he made her laugh and actually Sheena started to think, 'When did I last laugh with David? He's always at work', and she grew a bit resentful. David's friend asked Sheena out for a meal one night after one of the meetings. 'David won't mind,' he said. Sheena, feeling resentful of the lack of fun she and David had had recently, thought, 'Well he probably wouldn't notice anyway', and the resentment grew.

The day before she was due to go out for the meal, Sheena lay in bed and felt lonely. David lay next to her, but she seemed so distant from him, she didn't even feel she could reach out and touch him. A slow feeling of panic grew inside her as she realized she had lost the feeling of confidence in David's love for her. Something or someone had got in the way. Sheena prayed (something she hadn't done for a while), a desperate prayer asking God to help her understand what was happening. As she prayed she became convinced that she shouldn't go out for the meal, 'What was she thinking!' and that she and David really needed to talk this through. Sheena felt the confidence returning, as she knew she'd put God once again in control of her life and she trusted Him to protect her and David. They would definitely talk today.

## A person or a thing

An intruder can be a person or a thing. In the story above, it was David's friend; a person. The cricket that David was watching too much of and the meetings that Sheena was going to also became intruders even though they were not people, but things.

Once our focus comes off God and then in turn, each other, a gap starts to appear in our relationship. If you think of the triangle picture, the further we go from the  top of the triangle, so the wider the gap **A three-stranded rope** becomes between each other and it's then that intruders can enter between us. Sometimes we put the intruders there without realizing it, but sometimes they will break in themselves. Remember the definition in the dictionary.

## No complacency

God wants us to be sewn into that a three-stranded rope with Him. He wants us to speak to Him continually, asking for His protection and knowing His will for us together. We need to be aware of this and constantly put it into action. The devil wants to destroy marriage; remember the serpent in the Garden of Eden. We need to make sure we don't take each other for granted and become complacent with each other. God created marriage and delights in it, He will protect our marriages as we walk closely with Him and each other.

 **Spice it up**

• Pray together and ask God to show you areas where you may be living too separately from your spouse.

• Ask God to be the centre of your marriage.

• Talk to each other about your lives at the moment and take each other seriously if you suspect there may be an intruder.

**Spice from the Word**
*Matthew 11 vs. 28-30*

Jesus had a double yoke, two bullocks sharing the weight of the same burden, as a picture for his listeners. The yoke kept the two bullocks together. Jesus also promises that when we are yoked to Him, although we may be 'ploughing' through a heavy or frustrating time, He takes the strain from us and gives 'rest'. Keep yoked to one another and to Him.

# Memory Value

*Early on in our marriage, I watched Multibhai an eighty five year old friend sitting under the mango tree day after day. She didn't seem to be doing anything and that disturbed me. How could she just sit there, yet she seemed so tranquil, her sari wrapped around her plump old shoulders and a smile touching the corners of her mouth. 'What are you doing, Agi?' I asked, 'Praying Ruthie, and remembering.'*

## Take Time to Remember

Our lives were full of action, people, each other, babies, plans, future but Multibhai had taught us something. It was this: take time to remember. In *Deuteronomy 6* Moses exhorts the people, 'Then watch yourselves LEST YOU FORGET the Lord who brought you from the land of Egypt and out of the house of slavery.' The children of Israel were commanded to remember events, customs, deliverances, and the Lord's loving kindness constantly.

## Confidence for the future

*Memories of the past often give us confidence for the future, especially when the present may seem bleak.*

Rebecca and Ashok were going through a very bleak time. Ashok had lost his job and was feeling depressed. He was spending hours playing computer games at home to keep occupied. Rebecca felt frustrated that he was not doing more to get another job and kept nagging him. This started a vicious circle of blame and guilt. They were telling a close friend how miserable life was when he suddenly said, 'Hey, you two used to have great times together, tell me some of the best times.'

**They looked back to great times together**

Ashok said later that evening was a turning point. They looked back to great times together, a holiday in Goa, the birth of their twin boys, celebrations, evening walks, embarrassing moments, hilarious jokes, days when the Lord touched their lives powerfully, times when money was tight but a gift came with amazing timing. Remembering the past put them on track for the future again. There was hope. It was that hope which encouraged Ashok to look for another job.

## Making Memories

In our marriage we need to keep alert to 'memory value'. Often the best memories are built on spur of the moment decisions. This involves choice. At times the easiest thing to do in the evening is flop into a chair or watch TV. Then someone may say, 'It's a full moon, let's go out, take a meal and have a moonlight picnic.'

There is a beautiful beach at Mahabalipuram where we lived for seven years. Some of our favorite memories as a family are evenings. around a fire cooking fish and munching bread. Listening to the waves, watching the stars and trying to eat baked fish without swallowing bones and mouthfuls of sand by moonlight! Building memories establishes richer security and trust with each other.

How about encouraging certain family celebration traditions? For example a wedding anniversary is an excellent opportunity for this. Rod and I usually try to take a night away on our own anniversary, just to spoil each other in every way we can. Letting one another be our greatest star! We have a tradition of playing what we call the anniversary game. Here it is. Three questions I ask Rod:

1. What was my happiest moment this year?
2. What was my worst moment this year?
3. What was my best gift this year?

After racking his brain, he tells me what he thinks, and as he does all sorts of thoughts tumble around as we chat over the year. He asks me the same questions. We often don't hit the jackpot with the right answer but have found it a great way of stirring memories and keeping in touch with what's important to each other.

## Powerful Triggers

Listening to 'our song', looking through photo albums together, sorting through letters, meeting up with friends and even being able to cry together. Because it's true that some memories are sad. July 2nd is a date like that for us. It's the date when our first baby boy was born and died at the end of our first year of marriage. I remember one day ten years later when we took our children to visit the tiny grave in Kotagiri, Nilgiri Hills. As the sun burst through the early morning mist over the tea gardens, I looked at the four amazing children God had given us by then, and laughed through my tears. ***Memories and powerful triggers to remind us of our commitment to each other and faithfulness of Father God through whatever comes around the next corner.***

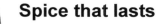

### Spice that lasts

Make a memory: contact some old friends, plan a visit to your 'honeymoon spot', get out the photo album. Take time to read through chapters of the book of Exodus together, choose a paraphrased version (The Message or The Living Bible). Let the story grip you. God's faithfulness to His chosen people never let them down. This same God is yours forever, remember that.

### Spice from the Word
*Luke 10 vs.38-42*

Mary had an unforgettable encounter with Jesus, taking time out to be with Him. A memory to last for a lifetime. Jesus rebukes Martha for trying to do the right thing at the wrong time. Rushing through life, being overorganized she missed what really mattered.

# Spiced Head to Foot

*'Pray for me!'*

*'OK',*

*'Lord help him/ her… um… Amen'*

Sometimes our praying for each other is limited to a quick Amen prayer just before a crucial meeting, or when we are sick, in a crisis, or just off to an interview for a new job or about to meet the Boss. We find ourselves getting into a rut, praying along the same well-worn 'bullock-cart' track.

> *Rod spent his childhood in an Indian village surrounded by sugar-cane fields, where his father worked as a doctor. Each evening as the sun was setting the bullock-carts would return from the fields piled high with juicy canes. Rod and his brothers would race each other to tug at a piece of cane, pull one off and chew on the delicious sugar with juices dripping down their chins. Often the bullocks would be driverless; having made deep worn ruts along the road they instinctively took the same track night after night.*

Try this week's spice to get the wheels of prayer rolling again along a fresh path. These 'Head to Foot' scripture based prayers will help you in your most important task as a husband or wife, praying for each other.

 ## Spice from the Word
*Song of Songs 5 vs.2-8*

The relationship we read about in Song of Songs is rich and finely tuned, but the seeds of destruction are there. They must be dealt with. It is not good to fall into a settled way of life without seeking anything new in our walk with the Lord or our marriage partner. All spiritual and marital progress must involve change from the present state, however good it may be. We do this by being 'spiced from head to foot'.

# For Him
## His Head
Lord, thank you for giving me my husband. You are his head, *1 Corinthians 11 v.3.*

## His Mind
Your plan for him is Christ Himself, and in Him are contained all the treasures of wisdom and knowledge, *Colossians 2 vs.2-3.* Capture all his thoughts to obey Christ, *2 Corinthians 10 v.5.* I pray that he will receive what Christ is teaching him and let His words enrich his life and make him wise, *Colossians 3 v.16.*

## His Eyes
Open his eyes that he may truly see from Your perspective, *2 Kings 6 v.17.* Give him wisdom to see clearly and really understand who Christ is and all that He did for him. Flood his heart with Your light so that he can see the future You have called us to share, *Ephesians 1 vs.17-18.*

## His Ears
Father, Your word says that faith comes by hearing and hearing by your word, *Romans 10 v.17.*

I pray that my husband will hear Your words with His heart, not just his head, *Psalm 78 v.1.*

## His Mouth
Give him Your words so that he may boldly make Jesus known, *Ephesians 6 v.9.*

Give him Your words so that he may know what to say to everyone, *Isaiah 50 v.4.*

Let the words of his mouth and the meditation of his heart be acceptable to You, *Psalm 19 v.14.*

## His Bones
Bring health to his body and nourishment to his bones as he fears You, rejects evil, and keeps

himself from bitterness, *Job 21 vs.23-25, Proverbs 3 vs.7-8*.

Guide him continually, Lord, and strengthen him, so that he will be like a watered garden, a spring of water which does not fail, *Isaiah 58 v.11*.

## His Heart

Thank You for Your promise: 'A new heart I will give him, and a new spirit I will put within him', *Ezekiel 36 vs.26-37*. I pray that he will let the peace of God rule his heart, *Colossians 3 v.15*.

May he be able to feel and understand how long, how wide, how deep, and how high you love us and to experience this love for himself, although it is so great that he will never reach the end of it. Fill him up with You, God, *Ephesians 3 vs.17-19*.

## His Hands

You want men everywhere to pray with holy hands lifted to You, free from sin, anger, and resentment, *1 Timothy 2 v.8*.

## His Legs

Help him lay aside every weight and the sins that seek to make him fall, so he can run with patience the race that You have set before him, *Hebrews 12 v.1*.

## His Feet

The steps of a good man are directed by You. Thank You that You delight in each step that he takes, *Psalm 37 v.23*.

Help us to walk together in the light of Jesus, *1 John 1 v.7* Help us to live in complete harmony with the attitude of Christ toward each other, *Romans 15 v.5*, as You give Your patience, faithfulness, and encouragement, *Ecclesiastes 9 v.9*.

By Your mighty power at work in my husband and me, You are able to do far more than I could ask or even dream - beyond my highest prayers, desires, hopes, or thoughts. I praise You and give You glory, *Ephesians 3 vs.20-21*.

Amen

# For Her

## Her Spirit
By Your gracious Spirit within her, grow in her life Your delicious fruit, love, joy, peace, patience, kindness, goodness, faithfulness, gentleness and self-control, *Galatians 5 vs.22-23*.

## Her Mind
Lord, open her mind to see You in Your word and reveal Your truth to her, *Luke 24 v.45*. Remind her to think about everything she has to praise You for in all things, *Philippians 4 v.8*.

## Her Eyes
Keep her eyes firmly fixed on You Lord, *Hebrews 12 v. 2*. You are the Way, the Truth and the Life, *John 14 v.6*. Help her to watch out for sly attacks from the enemy, *1 Peter 5 v. 8*.

## Her Ears
I pray that my wife will receive Your instruction, *Psalm 78 v.1*. May she be sensitive to Your gentlest whisper of guidance, *Isaiah 30 v.21*.

## Her Mouth
Open many doors for her to share the good news of Jesus freely, fully, and clearly. May she make the most of every opportunity as Your ambassador, *2 Corinthians 5 v.20*.

Remind her not to say hurtful or judgmental things about other people, but to say only what is wholesome and helpful for building others up according to their needs, *Ephesians 5 v.19*.

## Her Heart
Draw her close to Your heart, so that You alone will fill her heart to make her pure and true, *James ch 4 v.8*.

Create in my wife that new, clean heart filled with pure thoughts and right desires, *Psalm 51 v10*.

See to it that no root of bitterness grows in her heart and causes trouble in her relationships, *Hebrews ch 12 v.15*.

## Her Hands

I pray that she will continue to bless You as long as she lives, lifting up her hands to You in prayer, *Psalm 63 v.4*. As You direct her, may she open her hands to the needy, *Proverbs ch 31 v.20*.

## Her Legs

Help her to lay aside every weight and the sins that would cause her to fall, so that she can run with patience the race that You have set before her, *Hebrews ch 12 v.1*.

## Her Bones

Strengthen her body, so that she will be like a well-watered garden, an unfailing spring, *Isaiah 58 v.11*.

## Her Feet

Thank You for lifting her out of discouragement when things get tough. Set her feet on a firm, sure path with You, *Psalm 40 v 2, Psalm 66 v 9*. Delight in every step she takes. Direct her confidently, *Psalm 37 v.23*.

## Her Character

A good wife is worth more than jewels. Give her joy as she serves our family. Give her wisdom and grace in all business dealings. May she enjoy the respect of others because the fear of God is upon her life, *Proverbs 31 vs.1031, 1 Peter 3 v.4*.

Let me praise her and love her as Christ loves His bride, the church, and unselfishly give myself for her, so that she might be holy and blameless before You, *Ephesians 5 vs.28-29*.

I give You all glory in our lives, God, who by Your mighty power at work in us is able to do far more than we could dare to ask or dream, far beyond our highest prayers, desires, thoughts, or hopes, *Ephesians 3 vs.20-21*.

In Jesus' name,

Amen

# Resource Materials

Atkins Anne
*Split Image*
Hodder and Stoughton, 1987 & 1998

Biscoe Stuart
Pulling Together when pulling apart
Cook Communications Ministries,
International, Feb 1991

Cunningham David and Janet
Drink Drink your fill of Lovers

Dr Crab Larry
The Marriage Builder
Zondervan Publishing Company, 1992

Dr Prashantam BJ
Indian Case Studies in Therapeutic
Counselling

Gilbert Ruthie
Families are fun
Select Books 1995

Gillogly H & B
Achieving God's Design for Marriage
Joy Publishing

Hamp Diane
Excellence in Marriage

Harley WF
Love Busters
Fleming and Revell Company, 1997

Hill Craig
Marriage Covenant or Contract

Hongham John and Janet
Touch of Love

Huggett Joyce
Confflct – Friend or Foe
Kingsway, 1984

Huggett Joyce
Two into One
Inter-Varisity Press, 1981 & 1987

Hybels Bill & Lynn
Fit to be Tied
Harper Paperbacks, 1994

Kirk Mary
Marriage Work Out Book
Albatross Books, 1996

LaVonne Neff
One of a Kind: making the most of your
child's uniqueness
Multmomah Publishers Inc, 1988

Lowndes Leiel
How to Talk to Anyone
Harper Collins Publishers, 1999

Mc Dowell Josh
The Secret of Loving

Moir A & B
Why Men Don't Iron
Citadel Press, 10/2000

Stanley Lilian
Jolly Family

Storkey Elaine
Men Created or Constructed

Stott John RW
The Message of Romans
InterVarsity Press, July 2001

Warren Gillian Hang on I need to say
Something
Harpenden-Gazelle, 1997

12343607R00094

Made in the USA
Charleston, SC
28 April 2012